Oxford School Shakespeare

Romeo and Juliet

edited by
Roma Gill, OBE
M.A. *Cantab.* B.Litt. *Oxon.*

Oxford University Press

Oxford   Toronto   Melbourne

Oxford University Press, Great Clarendon Street, Oxford OX2 6DP

Oxford New York
Athens Auckland Bangkok Bogota Bombay
Buenos Aires Calcutta Cape Town Dar es Salaam Delhi
Florence Hong Kong Istanbul Karachi
Kuala Lumpur Madras Madrid Melbourne
Mexico City Nairobi Paris Singapore
Taipei Tokyo Toronto Warsaw

and associated companies in
Berlin Ibadan

Oxford is a trade mark of Oxford University Press

© Oxford University Press 1982
Reprinted 1982, 1984 (twice), 1985, 1986, 1987 (twice), 1989, 1990, 1991, 1992
Revised edition first published 1992
Reprinted 1992 (twice), 1993, 1994 (twice), 1995, 1996, 1997 (twice), 1998
Trade edition first published 1994
Reprinted 1996, 1997 (twice), 1998

ISBN 0 19 831986 X (Trade edition) 3 5 7 9 10 8 6 4 2
ISBN 0 19 831972 X (School edition) 3 5 7 9 10 8 6 4 2

Illustrations by Shirley Tourret

Cover photograph by Zoe Dominic shows Michael Thomas as Romeo, and Janet Maw as Juliet, in the Prospect Theatre Company's 1979 production of *Romeo and Juliet*.

To Luke

Oxford School Shakespeare
edited by Roma Gill

A Midsummer Night's Dream	Twelfth Night
Romeo and Juliet	The Taming of the Shrew
As You Like It	Othello
Macbeth	Hamlet
Julius Caesar	King Lear
The Merchant of Venice	Henry V
Henry IV Part I	The Winter's Tale
The Tempest	Antony and Cleopatra

Printed in Great Britain at the University Press, Cambridge

Contents

'a couple of unfortunate lovers'

This is the story of two lovers, who were secretly married and suddenly separated; and it involves a magic potion whose effects simulate death. It is an old story—much older than Shakespeare's play; the basic plot can be found as early as the third century A.D.[1] Much later, in the fifteenth century, European writers, chiefly Italian novelists, began to give it the details which we now recognize in Shakespeare's play. At first the Italians claimed that the events were contemporary and factual; even today tourists in Verona can be shown the tomb and balcony of Giulietta.

Montague and Capulet, the names of the two households involved in the action, are indeed historical.[2] But the individual characters, and the events of their lives are fictional. They were not, however, invented by Shakespeare.

Elizabethan audiences were in some ways more sophisticated than the audiences of the twentieth century. When we go to see a new play or (more likely) a new film, we expect to find the novelty in the action. Some of the situations may be familiar; we may be able to anticipate the ending; and the characters (who should not be *too* different from the people we meet every day) may speak lines that we have heard before in other plays and films. But we *do* demand a new story.

Shakespeare's audiences had different expectations. They were happy to be given stories that they recognized, so long as the dramatist's treatment was new and individual. It is possible to trace a source, or sources, for every one of Shakespeare's plays; and if we cannot do the same for all the plays by his contemporaries, it is probably because we have not yet looked in the right places! Some of Shakespeare's plays present very well-known stories—*Antony and Cleopatra*, for instance, or the range of plays dealing with the span of English history from the time of

---

1   In the *Ephesiaca* of Xenophon of Ephesus.

2   In the thirteenth century the Montecchi family lived in Verona, and the Capelletti in Cremona; Dante speaks of them as being responsible (partly) for the civil strife in Italy (*Purgatorio* VI).

Richard II to the reign of Henry VI. Shakespeare's researches were thorough: usually there is more than one source for a play. But this is not the case with *Romeo and Juliet.*

In this play Shakespeare relies almost entirely on a narrative poem, *The Tragicall History of Romeus and Juliet* by Arthur Brooke (published in 1562). The English poem is itself a translation of a popular prose fiction by Bandello (published 1554); and this in turn derives from even earlier Italian stories, especially one written by Luigi da Porto, who published his version of the legend in 1530, asserting its historical accuracy.

Shakespeare's play is not, however, a simple adaptation of Arthur Brooke's poem, although he follows his source closely in matters of detail as well as in the broad outlines of the plot. The relationship between poem and play is perhaps comparable to the relationship between *Romeo and Juliet* and the twentieth century musical *West Side Story.* In 1956 Jerome Robbins took the old legend and expressed it in the mood and idiom of his own day, turning Italian noblemen into New York street gangs, the Jets and the Sharks (Americans and Puerto Ricans). The Prince of Verona becomes a harassed police lieutenant. Robbins dealt freely with the material provided by Shakespeare's play; and in much the same way Shakespeare helped himself to portions of Brooke's poem and made whatever alterations he thought fit. In the Appendix you will find extracts from Shakespeare's source, so that you can compare them with the relevant parts of the play.

The dramatist speeds up the action: Brooke gives the lovers three months of married love, but Shakespeare permits only one night. Mercutio and Tybalt are little more than names in the poem; Shakespeare develops them into characters. The relationship between Juliet's Nurse and her foster-child is accounted for by Brooke in a single couplet, whereas in the play the Nurse is allowed the best part of a scene in which to demonstrate her affection for Juliet, before she is called upon to serve the purposes of the plot.

But the biggest difference is in the authors' attitudes to the lovers. Brooke, although he describes the situations with gusto, openly disapproves of the conduct of Romeo and Juliet whom he describes as:

> 'a couple of unfortunate lovers, thralling themselves to unhonest desire, neglecting the authority and advice of parents and friends, conferring their principal counsels with drunken gossips . . . attempting all adventures of peril for the attaining of their wished lust [and] abusing the honourable

name of lawful marriage. . . .[3]

Shakespeare, by contrast, is tender—often amused but always sympathetic: his contemporaries spoke of him as *'gentle* Shakespeare'.

His play was written (most probably) between 1594 and 1596 when he himself would be just over thirty years old—old enough to see the events in perspective, and young enough to understand. His understanding extends beyond the characters of his hero and heroine: it includes the Nurse—garrulous, bewildered, panic-stricken. And it takes in Mercutio, with all his vitality, as well as Friar Laurence who (although things go sadly wrong) is motivated by the best intentions in the world—to make peace, and to use love to conquer hate.

3   From a prose address 'To the Reader' at the beginning of his book.

Leading characters in the play

Montague Family

Old Montague and Lady Montague

The parents of Romeo. They have no part in the action of the play, but they illustrate the family feud with the Capulets. Old Montague is still eager to draw his sword and join in the fighting.

Romeo

Their only son. At the beginning of the play he thinks that he is in love with Rosaline, a lady whom we never see. It is the *idea* of being a lover that appeals to Romeo. He quickly forgets Rosaline when he meets Juliet. He is impulsive and passionate: he falls in love with Juliet and marries her. When his friend is killed by Juliet's cousin, Romeo avenges the murder—and as a punishment he is banished from his native city of Verona and his newly-married wife.

Benvolio

One of Romeo's friends. He is quite a serious young man, who is sympathetic to Romeo's passions, and who allows Romeo and Mercutio to tease him. He is a necessary character rather than an interesting one: he is always available to offer an explanation.

Mercutio

Romeo's other friend. He is full of energy, which is shown in the way he uses words, always playing with two or more meanings in a single word. His vitality leads him to challenge Tybalt, Juliet's cousin, to fight a duel. In the fighting, Mercutio is (almost accidentally) killed.

Capulet Household

Old Capulet and Lady Capulet

These two characters, the parents of Juliet, are more important than their counterparts, Romeo's parents. Old Capulet is anxious for his daughter to make a good marriage, but he is also—at the beginning of the play—insistent that she should love the man she marries. After the death of his nephew Tybalt, Old Capulet changes in his attitude to Juliet's marriage, and is prepared to force her to marry the man of his choice, Paris.

Lady Capulet is an obedient wife: she puts her husband's will before her daughter's wishes.

Juliet Their only child; we learn that other children have been born to the Capulets, but they have died. Juliet is almost fourteen years old. When the play opens she has never thought about marriage, but she is prepared to obey her parents and look with favour on the man they have chosen for her husband, the County Paris. But when she meets Romeo, Juliet falls in love with him, although she knows that his family and hers are deadly enemies.

Tybalt Juliet's cousin. Like Mercutio, he is full of energy; but (unlike Mercutio) he has no sense of fun. He is jealous of the family honour, and proud of his own skill in fencing. In the duel he kills Mercutio; and he is himself killed by Romeo.

Juliet's Nurse When Shakespeare wrote his play, it was not fashionable for noble ladies (like Lady Capulet) to feed their own infants. Instead, they gave the baby to a peasant woman who had recently given birth to a child and who had plenty of healthy milk in her breasts. Such a woman would nurse (i.e. feed) the child for three or four years; and it is likely that she would develop a maternal affection for the child, as though it were indeed her own.

Juliet's Nurse has such an affection for Juliet—strengthened, probably, by the fact that her own daughter, Susan, is dead (see *Act 1*, Scene 3, lines 18ff). She is eager to assist Juliet in her secret marriage, but after Tybalt's death she is bewildered and frightened. She is a simple woman, in whom piety and strong sexuality are combined with commonsense and a desire to please.

Escalus Prince of Verona, the ruler of the city in which the action takes place. Although he must try to be impartial, he is not indifferent to the feud between the Montagues and the Capulets, since he has relatives on both sides (both Mercutio and Paris are his kinsmen).

The Count Paris A nobleman, endowed with all the qualities that should make him an ideal husband for Juliet.

Friar Laurence A friar of the Order of Saint Francis. His good intentions in fact precipitate the tragedy.

Romeo and Juliet: commentary

Most of the play takes place (as the Chorus explains) in 'fair Verona'—an attractive little city in the north of Italy. The action moves swiftly from the city streets to the hall of Old Capulet's house, to the orchard below Juliet's balcony, to Friar Laurence's lonely cell, and finally to the vault where the ancestors of the Capulets are entombed. The Elizabethan stage had no curtains, and of course the theatre sold no programmes, so the characters themselves tell us where they are; they even indicate the time of day. The play starts on a Sunday morning in the middle of July; less than five days later—just before dawn on the following Thursday—it is all over.

Prologue

The Chorus—a single figure—appears on stage. He is not a character and has no personality. His function is simply to explain the situation, telling us that we are now in Verona, and that this is a city divided by civil war between two noble families. Their quarrel is an old one, an 'ancient grudge'. We never learn its cause: it seems to have become a habit for the Capulets and the Montagues to hate each other. But if we cannot know the cause of the quarrel, we can be warned of its cure.

When Shakespeare wrote *Romeo and Juliet* it was not unusual for a dramatist to introduce his play in this manner. The words of the Chorus would silence a restless audience, and settle the spectators into an appropriate mood for the first scene.

Act 1

Scene 1 Sunday morning. It is not yet nine o'clock, and two of Capulet's servants, Sampson and Gregory, have nothing very much to do as they wander through the streets of Verona. They tease each other, but when they see two of Montague's servants approaching, their good-natured rivalry is converted to hostility. All the servants are cowards, however, and can only exchange rude words and gestures until the Montague servants are given confidence by the arrival of Benvolio. Then Sampson issues the first challenge: 'Draw, if you be men'. Benvolio's attempts to make peace are frustrated by the arrival of Tybalt; at once the young noblemen are engaged in the fighting. Citizens of Verona rush to take sides, some urging a truce, some encouraging the Montague faction, and others joining the Capulet party: 'Strike! Beat them down! Down with the Capulets! Down with the Montagues!' Immediately the heads of the two families appear on the scene. Old Capulet calls for his 'long-sword'—a heavy, old-fashioned weapon that would have had no effect against the modern rapiers used by the younger generation. For a moment the two wives, Lady Capulet and Lady Montague, try to restrain their husbands, but their efforts are unnecessary. The Prince has arrived.

Escalus, Prince of Verona, is the representative of law and order in the play. His commands are obeyed, and his threats disperse the crowd. But we have seen enough to realize the gravity of the situation. In fewer than a hundred lines Shakespeare has created an atmosphere of tension where the least word or gesture can trigger off unthinking violence which is shared by the entire community—old and young alike, whether they are the lowest servants or the respected heads of noble families.

With the departure of the Prince, the mood of the scene changes. Lady Montague asks the question that the audience wants to ask: 'O where is Romeo? Saw you him today?' We have seen war; and now we hear about love, as Benvolio describes the behaviour of his infatuated friend. Romeo is up before dawn, walking alone in the woods and weeping; when the sun rises, he hurries home, locks himself in his room, and shuts out the daylight. These are the early symptoms of unrequited love, although neither Benvolio nor Romeo's parents appear to recognize this.

We wait for Romeo to show us the extent of his love-sickness. Romeo is miserable—we can have no doubt about that. We can be equally sure, however, that he *enjoys* his misery. He knows that there has been some kind of disturbance in the streets, but he is not interested. What matters to Romeo is the emotion that he calls 'love'. It makes him happy—and at the same time it makes him sad. He tries to express these two conflicting states in a series of witty paradoxes—phrases which seem absurd, and where the meaning of one word contradicts the sense of the word to which it is linked:

Feather of lead, bright smoke, cold fire, sick health.

He expects Benvolio to be amused, but Benvolio is a solemn young man and offers sympathy to his friend. Romeo welcomes the sympathy: it gives him an opportunity to talk even more about himself and his feelings—and this gives us the information that we need about his state of mind.

Romeo believes himself to be in love, but the woman he loves takes no interest in him. He describes her to Benvolio and tells us that she is perfect; but we can learn no more. (From the next scene we discover that her name is Rosaline and that she is a Capulet.) We can safely conclude, however, that this is only a young man's fancy, and a kind of sickness that could probably be cured if Romeo would follow Benvolio's prescription and 'Examine other beauties'.

He will soon be able to do this.

Scene 2   Old Capulet has returned home after his talk with the Prince, and he seems to be reconciled to the idea that he and Old Montague should start to live at peace with each other. He has important business to deal with. The County Paris is eager to make Juliet his wife. Capulet is a *good* father and Juliet is his only child. There have been other children, but they are dead: 'Earth hath swallow'd all my hopes but she'. This must make Juliet very precious to him and he is reluctant to lose her. However, if she should fall in love with Paris, her father will be happy to give his consent to the marriage.

That evening (it is still Sunday) Old Capulet will hold 'an old accustom'd feast'—an elaborate ball which will be attended by all the nobility of Verona. It is a regular event, and the message that Capulet now sends to his guests is probably not so much an invitation as a reminder.

The servants in the first scene speak in plain, simple prose.

Benvolio and Tybalt speak a flexible blank verse—that is to say, verse where the regular stresses of the iambic pentameter fit in with the formal rhythms of speech. Prince Escalus, coming on to the stage at line 78, speaks a much more dignified blank verse; his is the kind of speech that is delivered from a platform. Romeo uses rhymes when he speaks of the nature of his love: the subject is 'poetic', and so it is appropriate that the verse should seem equally unreal—remote from everyday speech. In the second scene there is always a tendency for the lines to rhyme in couplets, and the effect is to speed up the action: it is important that we should know about the feast, but there is no need for us at the moment to pay very close attention. The servant who carries Capulet's invitation speaks in prose. This is not the same kind of prose as that spoken by Sampson and Gregory in the first scene; Shakespeare's contemporaries would recognize this passage as being a parody of a kind of ornate prose that was fashionable in the last decade of the sixteenth century. It is a comic moment, and the scene continues with comedy (and often with rhymed couplets) as Romeo and Benvolio learn about the Capulet ball and Benvolio makes a suggestion.

Scene 3   The couplets give way to blank verse again as the scene changes once more. We are inside the Capulet house again, this time awaiting an introduction to Juliet. She stands quiet and obedient whilst her Nurse—the foster-mother who has cared for her since the day that she was born—remembers incidents in the child's life. At the beginning of the scene Lady Capulet dismisses the Nurse: 'Nurse, give us leave awhile. We must talk in secret.' But immediately the Nurse is recalled: 'Nurse, come back again. I have remember'd me, thou's hear our counsel.' The Nurse, we realize, is not an ordinary servant; she is almost a member of the family. When she begins to tell us about Juliet's childhood we learn not only Juliet's age (although this is very important) but also a great deal about the character of the Nurse. She has known personal sorrow in the death of her daughter, Susan, but she is philosophical about this: 'Well, Susan is with God; She was too good for me.' She remembers trivial details; her speech is repetitive; and she cannot continue a line of thought for very long. Lady Capulet is a complete contrast. She asks a direct question: 'Tell me, daughter Juliet, how stands your disposition to be married?' Juliet's answer is evasive: 'It is an honour that I dream not of'; after all, she is not yet fourteen. But her mother persists: 'Well, think of marriage now'. She introduces the subject of Paris and his proposal of marriage. Her description of Paris is no doubt intended to recommend the gentleman to her daughter, but the extended metaphor (spread over eleven lines of verse) has no effect upon *our* emotions. Juliet's reply shows only a young girl's obedience.

The arrival of the servants with the information that 'the guests are come', breaks into the strained formality, and we are made aware that time has been passing. It is now Sunday evening. Lady Capulet responds to the servant's request and leaves the stage in order to receive her guests at supper. She is followed by Juliet and the Nurse.

Scene 4   Their departure does not leave the stage empty for long. Romeo enters (at the opposite side). He is accompanied by Mercutio and Benvolio. As well as the three close friends, there are other gentlemen in the party. They are all disguised—wearing fancy dress and comic masks to hide their faces. Attendants bear torches, and there are probably musical instruments—certainly there is a drum (line 114). Benvolio has organized a *masquerade*—an amateur entertainment, fashionable in the sixteenth century, in which gentlemen could visit a party to which they had not been invited. After making a speech to the host (the speech referred to by Benvolio in the first line of the scene) the gentlemen dance, flirt with the ladies, pay compliments to the host, and then depart. The host regarded the arrival of masquers as a form of flattery, not in any sense an intrusion into the privacy of his party.

Throughout the scene we are constantly made aware of the fact that it is dark; night has fallen, and torches must be used to give the illusion of darkness. Benvolio and Mercutio are full of enthusiasm for the masquerade. Romeo is reluctant to join them, because he would prefer to be alone with his love-sick misery and because he has a strong sensation of impending disaster: 'I dream'd a dream tonight'. But before Romeo's dream can threaten to spoil the light-hearted fun of the scene, Mercutio's energetic imagination explodes into life with his fantastic 'Queen Mab' speech.

The speech is sheer invention. It has no particular relevance to the action of the play—except to allow enough time for Capulet's guests to eat their supper. The speech has to be enjoyed for itself. There is no deeply significant meaning.

Before the masquers leave the stage Romeo voices his unease, and then resigns himself to fate.

Scene 5 The stage is now filled with activity as the Capulet servants rush about, moving furniture and dishes as a clear indication that the meal is over and that the dancing is about to begin. Once again we are inside Capulet's house.

Old Capulet is a jovial host and welcomes the masquers in a happy mood, recalling the masquerades that he himself took part in when he was a young man. The masquers mix with the guests in the dance; two old men (Capulet and his cousin) chat about their acquaintances; and Romeo catches sight of Juliet.

Romeo is overwhelmed by Juliet's beauty. But whilst he stands in wonder he is observed by Tybalt, who recognizes him as an enemy. Tybalt's reaction is immediate: a foe means a fight. Fortunately Old Capulet is watching, and we see that the older man has become a little wiser since this morning. He restrains Tybalt—but we realize that his restraint will not be effective for very long.

The altercation between Capulet and his nephew has given Romeo time to approach Juliet, and we must imagine the two lovers standing quite apart from the rest of the characters on stage. The dancing continues, but they are not a part of it. Their separateness is emphasized by the form of the verse in which they have begun to speak. Romeo starts with devout religious utterance:

> If I profane with my unworthiest hand,
> This holy shrine. . . .

He develops the religious image for four lines which rhyme alternately (ABAB), then Juliet picks up the same image, speaking the next four lines in the same pattern (with rhyme CBCB). A third quatrain is shared between the two (rhyme DEDE) and a final couplet is spoken—the first line by Juliet, the second by Romeo, who clearly takes advantage to kiss Juliet at the end of his line.

> Then move not, while my prayers' effect I take.

The fourteen lines are in fact a sonnet—a complex and highly artificial verse form, popular in the sixteenth century and generally regarded as the proper medium for love poetry. The form is used to emphasize the lovers' isolation from the society in which they live; and the way in which they share the same extended image and same verse form emphasizes the harmony of their thoughts. Even so, we must notice that Juliet manages to tease Romeo a little within the solemn expression of devotion. After the kiss, it appears that the lovers are about to start a second sonnet; but this is interrupted by the Nurse.

Now the lovers must be brought back from the state of isolation to the real world; and they must begin to understand what has happened to them. The Nurse chats to Romeo and answers his question in a very down-to-earth way as she explains that Juliet is the daughter of the host and that the man who 'can lay hold on her Shall have the chinks' (i.e. he will be rich). It is time for the masquerade to end.

And now Juliet must learn the truth. Once again the Nurse is the source of information. The last lines of the scene combine ordinary speech with formal rhymed couplets. Juliet's mind, we can see, is working on two levels of thought: her questions to the Nurse are naturalistic, but her inner thoughts—spoken for the hearing of the audience alone—are prophetic.

Chorus   'The use of this Chorus is not easily discovered.' These are the words of one of the first and greatest of Shakespeare's editors, Dr Samuel Johnson, who was writing in the eighteenth century. He complained that the information given in the speech is unnecessary; and indeed it is! But look at the play from the point of view of an actor—the actor playing the part of Romeo. He has just performed an intense love-duet, and then brought the character to a terrifying appreciation of the dangers of Romeo's position. He leaves the stage in *Act 1*, Scene 5 at line 126; the scene ends less than twenty lines later. *Act 2*, Scene 1 demands Romeo's appearance at the very beginning. The fourteen lines (another sonnet) spoken by the Chorus are necessary to allow the actor to get his breath back, and perhaps even to dash round the back of the stage, and enter from the opposite side, so that the audience does not think he has returned to the ballroom.

Act 2

Scene 1   We now have to pay close attention to the words of the actors when they mention the location of the scenes that follow. Benvolio tells us that Romeo, after speaking two lines, has disappeared and 'leap'd this orchard wall'. Whilst Mercutio and Benvolio fool around on one side of the wall—outside the orchard—Romeo lurks on the other side, hearing Mercutio's jokes, but not responding.

Mercutio is in high spirits. He calls for his friend, pretending to be a magician who can raise the ghosts of the dead by mysterious invocations, calling on the name of a deity. He invokes Venus and Cupid, and then decides that Rosaline is the goddess whom Romeo worships—with sexual, not spiritual desire. Like the 'Queen Mab' speech, this display of verbal fireworks is delightful for itself; but it also presents two different aspects of love. We are reminded of Romeo's passion for Rosaline—the fanciful emotion that made him feel ill, yet which he indulged because (probably) he had nothing better to do. He worshipped Rosaline as a goddess. Mercutio's own attitude to women is in complete contrast; there is no emotion at all here, only sexual desire. We shall now be shown a third kind of love—one which has elements of the other two, but which is far more powerful than either of them.

Mercutio and Benvolio decide that they might just as well go home to bed, since they cannot find Romeo:

> 'tis in vain
> To seek him here that means not to be found.

Scene 2   The verse does not allow any break in the action; Romeo completes the couplet:

> He jests at scars, that never felt a wound.

We must, however, be aware that the setting has changed: we are now *inside* the orchard, and Romeo is looking up at the light shining through a window.

He begins to speak about his love for Juliet. At first there seems to be very little difference between *this* love, and the emotion he pretended to feel for Rosaline:

> Arise, fair sun, and kill the envious moon,
> Who is already sick and pale with grief,
> That thou her maid art far more fair than she.

This is the conventional language of love poetry: it was fashionable for lovers to speak in this way. Very quickly, however, the language becomes more simple; Romeo is learning to express genuine feelings:

It is my lady. O, it is my love!
O that she knew she were!

That second line is especially effective *because* it is incomplete—
there are three poetic 'feet' instead of five; we have become
accustomed to the rhythm of the pentameter, so we wait for the
completion of the line, and the silence indicates that Romeo cannot
find words to express his thoughts.

The Elizabethan stage had a small area (probably at the centre
back) which had curtains, and a roof supported by pillars. Actors
could come on to the main, open stage through the curtains; or
they could appear and act short scenes from the roof itself, which
supplied a second acting level. Now this becomes the balcony
outside Juliet's bedroom; Juliet comes out into the night, believing
that she is alone, and begins to speak of her love for Romeo.

Fear and delight are mingled in Juliet's heart. She has found a
'dear perfection' in Romeo's person, but she knows well that his
name is her enemy—because 'Romeo' is one of the family names of
the Montagues. Juliet is startled, even a little embarrassed, when she
realizes that Romeo has overheard her private thoughts, but soon the
two lovers are able to discuss their feelings with simple honesty. The
mood of the scene varies between intense passion and gentle teasing.
It is interrupted when the Nurse calls to Juliet from within—she is
off-stage, and we must imagine her to be waiting in Juliet's bedroom.
The effect is the same as that achieved in the ballroom scene, when
the lovers were drawn back from the isolation of their love into the
real world. After the interruption they renew their promises to each
other. Suddenly Juliet makes a proposal which must come as a
surprise (although a delightful one) to her new lover:

If that thy bent of love be honourable,
They purpose marriage, send me word tomorrow . . .
Where and what time thou wilt perform the rite;

Only a few moments before, Juliet had expressed her anxieties
about this new relationship: 'It is too rash, too unadvis'd, too
sudden'. Now she seems to have forgotten the worry, or else her
love has become so strong that she cannot restrain herself.

When the lovers have separated, and Juliet has returned to her
bedroom, Romeo is alone on the stage for a short time—just long
enough to tell us the time of day:

>The grey-ey'd morn smiles on the frowning night,
>Chequering the eastern clouds with streaks of light.

It is Monday morning.

Scene 3   The scene changes completely now, as we go ahead of Romeo to Friar Laurence's 'close cell'—the remote hermitage where the holy man devotes his time to prayer, study, and the concoction of medicines from the herbs that grow around his home. He delivers a short lecture on herbal drugs that can kill and cure; and once again this allows Romeo to travel from one location—the Capulet orchard at daybreak—to another: the friar's cell, where he arrives 'ere the sun advances his burning eye'.

He confesses everything to Friar Laurence, who is clearly accustomed to hearing Romeo's confessions of love and who has obviously given him sound advice in the past (which Romeo has ignored until now). Friar Laurence can see a way in which this new love of Romeo and Juliet—Montague and Capulet—could perhaps be turned to an even greater good. It might make peace between the two families: 'turn your households' rancour to pure love'.

Scene 4   After the solemn interview with the friar, the mood and scene of the play change completely. Back in the city of Verona Romeo's two friends, Benvolio and Mercutio are fresh and full of energy; presumably they have been able to sleep a little—and at least they have changed out of their masquerade costumes. Romeo, when he joins them at line 37, is still wearing fancy dress: Mercutio jokes about it—'Signor Romeo, *bon jour*! There's a French salutation to your French slop.'

Before Romeo appears, the two young men have been discussing Tybalt, the fierce nephew of Old Capulet who had tried to attack Romeo at the masquerade. Old Capulet's restraint has not lasted long: Tybalt has already, we hear, sent a letter to Romeo challenging him to fight a duel. Mercutio describes Tybalt, and again we hear the same excited imagination that presented Queen Mab to us. Mercutio laughs at Tybalt and his affectations—his correct fencing technique, his accent, and his fondness for using the latest slang expressions. At the same time, however, he has some respect: Tybalt is not to be taken lightly—he is 'More than Prince of Cats'. This passage serves to remind us of the character whom we met for a short time at Capulet's party, and to prepare us for his second appearance.

Romeo joins his friends, and all three engage in witty chatter; they are full of energy, and the outlet for this energy is (at the moment) verbal fighting in the best of friendly relationships. At the height of the fun, Juliet's Nurse appears. She is (we must assume) a fairly large woman, wearing a flowing dress. As she comes into view Romeo pretends that she is a ship: 'A sail! A sail!' The Nurse pretends to be shocked by the bawdy jokes; but she enjoys them. She delivers Juliet's message to Romeo in her rambling prose. Since we already know what the message is, we can concentrate on the comedy of the Nurse's speech. The action of the play is now moving very fast; it is still Monday, and the time is twelve noon.

Scene 5   For Juliet, however, the time seems to pass slowly; her Nurse has been away since nine o'clock, 'and from nine till twelve is three long hours'. More comedy follows when the Nurse returns with Romeo's greetings and instructions to his love, because the Nurse is in a mischievous mood and enjoys keeping Juliet in suspense. She encourages the girl's expectations:

> Your love says, like an honest gentleman,
> And a courteous and a kind and a handsome . . .

She can see that Juliet grows more excited with every word—and so she breaks off, ceasing her praise of Romeo to ask a plain question on quite another matter: 'Where is your mother?' The great news—that the marriage ceremony has been arranged—is communicated simply, mixed with the Nurse's complaints about the trials that she must undergo to serve the child she loves. She sends Juliet to the wedding—and she herself goes for her dinner.

Scene 6   At Friar Laurence's cell, the bridegroom waits eagerly for his bride; the friar's words of hesitation and foreboding do not diminish Romeo's delight, and very soon he is rewarded by the appearance of Juliet. A few brief words of love are spoken by each of the two before the friar hurries them off to his chapel, refusing to let them 'stay alone Till holy church incorporate two in one.'

Act 3

Scene 1   Italian summer afternoons are hot, and it is sensible to take a rest in
the shade, or even indoors. Benvolio recommends this to
Mercutio, pointing out that members of the Capulet family are
about in the streets, 'And if we meet we shall not 'scape a brawl'.
Mercutio responds with his usual good-natured humour, but his
invention seems slower than usual; probably he too feels hot and
rather tired. His energy is restored when Tybalt appears, in search
of Romeo and determined to fight. Mercutio is outraged when
Romeo receives Tybalt's abuse with mildness, and draws his own
sword to attack the Capulet.

Romeo tries to stop the fighting; his interference seems to
confuse Mercutio, and he fails to evade Tybalt's sword. We are
shown the accuracy of Tybalt's fencing, described earlier by
Mercutio: 'one, two, and the third in your bosom' (2, 4, 24). Even
at the point of death, Mercutio is witty. His wit, as much as his
curse on the houses of Montague and Capulet alike, awakens
Romeo's own sense of honour. For a moment he forgets his new
bride and takes his sword to attack her cousin in an act of
vengeance for the death of Mercutio.

Once again the citizens of Verona rush to the scene of the
fighting; and once again Prince Escalus appears and tries to
enforce peace. The first time that we saw this (*Act 1*, Scene 1) the
intervention came before any harm was done. This time it is too
late. Mercutio's body has been taken from the scene; but Tybalt
lies at Romeo's feet, and the blood-stained sword is in Romeo's
hand.

Prince Escalus hears of the sequence of events from
Benvolio's mouth, and he listens to the pleas of Lady Capulet and
Old Montague, who speak as representatives of the warring
families. Escalus promises strict justice: his first ruling is to banish
Romeo from Verona:

> Let Romeo hence in haste,
> Else, when he is found, that hour is his last.

He can do neither more nor less than this. Romeo has broken the
law and must be duly punished; otherwise, all civil law will break
down, and a state of anarchy will result:

> Mercy but murders, pardoning those that kill.

Scene 2   Ignorant of what is happening in Verona's streets, Juliet longs for night to come, when Romeo will 'Leap to these arms' untalk'd of and unseen'. She is passionately in love, with a physical longing to possess Romeo and to be possessed by him. She is in an ecstasy of impatience. But the Nurse shatters her dreams with the confused reports of death and banishment, Tybalt and Romeo. Juliet's heart and mind are torn by conflicting emotions as she struggles to understand what the Nurse is saying. At the end of the scene she subsides into grief for the loss of her husband, and sends the Nurse to seek for him at Friar Laurence's cell.

Scene 3   The Friar is trying to calm Romeo, preaching the virtue of stoic resignation to fate and pointing out that things might be worse. Romeo is condemned to banishment, not to death. But for Romeo, banishment from Verona means separation from Juliet; and this is worse than death. When the Nurse tells of Juliet's grief, Romeo's distress increases and he is ready to kill himself. The friar, however, has a plan; and after another lecture (which is much admired by the Nurse) he takes control of the situation.

Scene 4   So much has happened in such a short time that the characters themselves find it difficult to remember what day it is; Old Capulet has to ask Paris—'But, soft! What day is this?' It is still only Monday. Juliet has gone to bed, and Old Capulet himself 'would have been a-bed an hour ago' had it not been for the presence of the County Paris, who wants to know whether or not he can marry Juliet.

     Capulet reaches a sudden decision: Paris shall marry his daughter, and the wedding will be held that same week, on Thursday. It will not be a grand occasion, because the family is in mourning for the death of Tybalt: there will be 'some half a dozen friends, And there an end.'

     It is time for bed; in fact 'It is so very very late, That we may call it early by and by.'

Scene 5   For Romeo and Juliet it is far too early. Romeo has obeyed the friar, climbed the balcony to Juliet's bedroom, and consummated the marriage whose religious ceremony was performed on Monday afternoon. Without the physical consummation, the marriage would not have been complete; the vows would not be irrevocable—Romeo and Juliet would not have been man and wife.

     Now they must be separated. The birdsong they hear comes from the lark, the first bird to sing in the morning, and the light in the east heralds the rising sun. Romeo must save his life by escaping to Mantua.

The lovers' farewells are interrupted by the Nurse, warning that Lady Capulet is looking for her daughter. Romeo climbs down from the balcony and Juliet, standing above, imagines that she sees him, 'As one dead in the bottom of a tomb'.

Lady Capulet probably enters through the curtained area below Juliet's balcony; the restricted space of the upper acting-level would not be able to accommodate all the members of the Capulet family (including the Nurse) who are needed for the rest of the scene.

Juliet's mother is cold and unsympathetic. She does not understand her daughter's grief, of course, and naturally assumes that the tears are for Tybalt. Juliet's words deceive Lady Capulet, but their meaning is clear to the audience when she speaks of her anguish and her longing to be close to the man who murdered her cousin. She speaks politely to her mother, addressing her formally as 'Madam' and 'your ladyship', and appearing to be thankful for the promised 'day of joy' that is so unexpected. But when she learns of the nature of the celebration, Juliet forgets all her obedience and good manners. The news is a shock; obstinate refusal to marry Paris is the only possible reaction.

Juliet's father enters. His own distress at the death of his nephew turns to sympathy with what he believes to be Juliet's grief for Tybalt. But sorrow instantly turns to rage when he learns that Juliet has refused the offered marriage. He bullies and threatens, cursing his daughter and swearing at the Nurse. In a storm of anger he leaves the stage, followed by his wife, who, like him, has disowned their child: 'Do as thou wilt, for I have done with thee.'

Juliet demands comfort from her Nurse, whom she has loved and trusted for fourteen years. But the Nurse has no comfort to offer. She too has experienced grief and shock at the events of the previous day, and now she can only think of the most practical way of getting out of all their difficulties. No one knows about the marriage to Romeo; he is now banished and will never dare to return to Verona and claim Juliet as his wife. It would be so easy if Juliet were to forget about Romeo, and marry Paris—who, after all, is 'a lovely gentleman'.

Juliet is completely alone.

Act 4

Scene 1   Whilst the Capulet household is in an uproar of conflicting passions, the County Paris has acted quickly and efficiently; we find him with Friar Laurence, making arrangements for the wedding. He speaks gentle and affectionate words to Juliet when she appears, and Juliet replies with calm courtesy. When she is alone with the friar, however, Juliet gives way to her grief once more, threatening to kill herself rather than break the sacred vow she made to Romeo. Her passion becomes hysterical as she describes what she will suffer rather than marry Paris:

> chain me with roaring bears,
> Or hide me nightly in a charnel-house,
> O'er-cover'd quite with dead men's rattling bones . . .

Friar Laurence can offer a solution—although even this is not free from fear and danger. His researches into the medicinal qualities of herbs have enabled him to concoct a 'distilled liquor' which Juliet must drink. She will fall into a coma, and her body will have every appearance of death. She will be laid in the family vault, and there she will sleep until Romeo, recalled from Mantua by Friar Laurence, comes to rescue her.

Scene 2   The conference with Friar Laurence is reassuring, and when Juliet returns home she is able to ask her father's forgiveness. We find Old Capulet in a state of excitement, preparing for the wedding: he seems to have forgotten that he had decided to invite only 'some half a dozen friends' (3, 4, 27)—now he is asking for 'twenty cunning cooks'. Pleased with Juliet's new obedience, he decides to have the wedding one day early: 'We'll to church tomorrow'.
   This is still Tuesday, but it is quite late: Lady Capulet points out that it is 'now near night' when she attempts to change her husband's mind, but Old Capulet is firm; he will take care of the preparations:

> I'll not to bed tonight. Let me alone;
> I'll play the housewife for this once.

Scene 3   Juliet and her Nurse have also been preparing for the wedding, choosing Juliet's best clothes and jewels. Now Juliet asks to be left alone. She is excited and frightened—perhaps the friar's drug is really a poison; perhaps she will wake up to find herself alone in the vault among the dead bodies. She is terrified; but she drinks the potion.

Scene 4 Very early in the morning—Old Capulet points out that ''tis three o'clock'—the servants are rushing around making preparations for the feast. The Nurse is sent to wake Juliet, and the bridegroom, the County Paris, has arrived to claim his bride. He has brought musicians with him, intending that they should wake Juliet and accompany the happy couple throughout the day. This has become quite a grand wedding, in the English style of the sixteenth century.

Scene 5 The curtains are drawn around Juliet's bed, and the Nurse chatters to her mistress, whom she is unable to see. The discovery is slow: Juliet is sleeping; she is fully dressed; she appears to be dead. Lady Capulet is called to the scene; then Juliet's father; and then Paris and Friar Laurence. A general lamentation follows, and each of the characters is allowed a short recitation of grief.

The scene is not an easy one to act. The audience cannot share the emotions expressed by the characters, because we know the truth: Juliet is not dead, and all this is unnecessary. We must save our tears—we shall need them later. To prevent undue audience involvement, Shakespeare gives the characters an exaggerated kind of verse; there are too many words, and they are too strong for us to pay much attention to their meaning. All four recitations start with a list of adjectives; the effect is *almost* comic—we find it difficult to sympathize with the father who expresses himself in this way:

Despis'd, distressed, hated, martyr'd, kill'd!
Uncomfortable time, why cam'st thou now
To murder, murder our solemnity?

Friar Laurence preaches a short funeral sermon and gives instructions for the removal of Juliet's body.

The musicians try to comprehend what is happening; they are not deeply involved, but they will wait for the mourners, and accompany them to the churchyard.

Act 5

Scene 1 Bad news travels fast, and that same day (Wednesday) Romeo is informed of the catastrophe that has befallen his bride and her family. He is safe in Mantua, but life has no meaning for him now. He describes an apothecary's shop, whose owner is so poor that he can be bribed to sell poison. The sale is completed, and Romeo leaves for Verona.

Scene 2 But Romeo was given the wrong information. We hear now how Friar John, who should have delivered a letter to Romeo, was prevented from leaving Verona. In this scene we cannot fail to realize that Shakespeare's time-scheme for *Romeo and Juliet* is too compressed; perhaps the dramatist was himself working at high speed when he condensed the nine months of Arthur Brooke's narrative action into a mere five days.

The short scene, however, allows Romeo to travel from Mantua to Verona, arriving outside the Capulet vault on Wednesday night.

Scene 3 Juliet's tomb already has a visitor—the County Paris, who has vowed to bring flowers and scented water to the grave every night. His ritual is interrupted by the arrival of Romeo, who proceeds to force open the tomb where he expects to find his wife's body.

Romeo is no longer the dreamy youth that we met at the beginning of the play. He describes himself as 'a desperate man' and, when Paris ignores his gentle warning, he fights with a serious determination which is totally different from the rough assaults of the servants (*Act 1*, Scene 1) and from the elegant sword-play of the young nobleman (*Act 3*, Scene 1). Romeo intends to kill Paris without ceremony and without delay.

He has no regrets when he has killed Paris, but he feels pity for the 'Good gentle youth'. He is preparing to lay Paris, tenderly, in the tomb when he looks on Juliet's face. Although he is prepared for death, he in fact sees life: 'beauty's ensign yet Is crimson in thy lips and in thy cheeks'. The audience knows that he is not deceived, and the tension is great. Juliet *might* wake in time; all might yet be well.

The hope is in vain, of course. Romeo drinks his poison, whose action is swift: he dies kissing Juliet, a second before Friar Laurence, stumbling in the graveyard, enters the tomb to comfort Juliet in her waking moments. Juliet seems refreshed after her sleep, but her resolution is not diminished. As soon as she understands the situation, she acts—first kissing the poison on Romeo's lips, then making sure of her death with Romeo's dagger, which she plunges into her own breast: 'O happy dagger! This is thy sheath!'

Once again the citizens of Verona are drawn to the scene, and Prince Escalus appears among them. Friar Laurence provides the narrative this time, freely confessing his own part in the events and offering himself for punishment. The County's Page and Balthasar fill in some missing details. Capulet and Montague join hands; they have paid a high price for their new friendship. There is not much to be said:

> A glooming peace this morning with it brings;
> The sun for sorrow will not show his head.

It is Thursday morning.

Art and Nature

It is very rarely possible to give a precise date for plays produced in the sixteenth and seventeenth centuries; it is generally agreed that *Romeo and Juliet* was written between 1594 and 1596— at much the same time that Shakespeare was working on *A Midsummer Night's Dream*. The two plays have a lot in common, and it could even be argued that the interlude of 'Pyramus and Thisbe' which is performed by amateur actors in *A Midsummer Night's Dream* is Shakespeare's own parody of romantic tragedies such as *Romeo and Juliet*.

The chart at the end of this book will show you how busy Shakespeare was during the last decade of the sixteenth century; he seems to have been intensely active during the middle years of the decade. It is as though his mind were overflowing with ideas. He had read a great deal, and he wanted to write. His reading included popular fiction, classical poetry (both in Latin and in English translation), the Bible, and works by his contemporaries in prose and poetry, as well as drama. During this period, poets and dramatists alike were experimenting with a variety of styles: blank verse was a new form, and so was the sonnet. Shakespeare experimented with both of these forms, and with many others; as you read through the Commentary on *Romeo and Juliet* you will see that I have tried to point out some of the different styles and explain the effects that I think Shakespeare was trying to achieve.

He is not *always* successful. This is a fairly early play, and Shakespeare has not yet acquired the skills that are developed in the great tragedies (*King Lear* and *Macbeth*, for example). But he often *does* succeed. I admire the love sonnet spoken by Romeo and Juliet at Capulet's ball, and I am very moved by Juliet's eager anticipation of her wedding-night, and by her terror before drinking the friar's potion. I believe that the Nurse's rambling account of Juliet's childhood and Mercutio's brilliant account of Queen Mab have no equals in the drama of this, or any other, period of English Literature.

Against these, however, we must balance the tediousness of Lady Capulet's description of the County Paris; Friar Laurence's sermons which (although the Nurse admires his philosophy) I find rather boring; and the curious mixture of pathos and farce when Juliet's 'death' is discovered by her family on the wedding morning.

Shakespeare is often careless too. The characters are very specific about the timing of events, and very careful to tell us about the location of scenes; but this becomes slightly confusing when we find that Romeo has rushed from Verona to Mantua and back again in less than two days, whilst Friar John has been unavoidably delayed for (apparently) a considerable time when he ought to have been in Mantua. There is even a lack of care sometimes in the words of the play; we cannot excuse (by calling it 'common Elizabethan usage') the grammar of lines 7–8 of the Chorus's first speech, where the singular verb 'Doth' comes uncomfortably with the plural subject 'overthrows'. And when the servants are bringing logs for the fire at Capulet's ball, we realize that Shakespeare has forgotten, in adapting Arthur Brooke's poem, that in the narrative the ball is held at Christmas; in his play he has transferred the action to July.

The faults as well as the virtues of *Romeo and Juliet* seem to me to indicate an enthusiastic playwright working under considerable pressure. He is experienced enough to know what the audience wants from him: excitement; romance; horror; bawdy jokes; low comedy; and sophisticated word-play. He is skilled enough to provide all these: the frequent sword-fights; young lovers who sacrifice all for love; scenes in a family vault at dead of night; Mercutio's witty conjuration of Romeo; servants who cannot draw their daggers without making puns; and the constant flow of *doubles entendres*, paradoxes, classical allusions, rhymes. . . .

Romeo and Juliet is a very artificial play—it was made by an artist. It is also the work of a craftsman, who had a sound knowledge of the resources and limitations of the theatre in which his play would be performed. With two acting levels, he could plan for a balcony scene; since there was no fixed scenery and nothing to interrupt the action, he could allow the characters to change place (from street to bedroom, from Verona to Mantua) without any break in the movement of the play—though he must always take care to write a reference to the place into someone's speech, so that the audience does not get lost. All performances in the public theatres took place in daylight—so for the night scenes Shakespeare makes sure that at least one character mentions the torches that the actors should be carrying.

Dr Johnson, the eighteenth-century editor, did not appreciate the second speech made by the Chorus which (as he said) 'conduces nothing to the progress of the play'. Dr Johnson was writing from his study: any actor, breathless after the ballroom scene and preparing for the big balcony scene that follows, could tell the scholar why these fourteen lines are necessary. Shakespeare was himself an actor (he is more likely to have played the part of Friar Laurence than that of Romeo) and he understood an actor's needs.

To satisfy contemporary audiences and actors is a considerable achievement for any dramatist at any time. It was especially difficult in the sixteenth century when the large audiences were made up of spectators from every level of society, with all kinds of interest and degrees of intelligence. What Elizabethan audiences did *not* expect—and what we today always look for—is the detailed, sensitive character-portrayal for which Shakespeare is most famous. No other dramatist of this period creates characters as Shakespeare does: their *dramatis personae* are types, Shakespeare's are individuals. The characters' vitality comes in part from the precise information we learn about them—information which is unnecessary to the plot of the play: we do not *need* to know that the Nurse's daughter was called Susan, or that her husband was 'a merry man'. And they speak in ways that vary subtly from one character to another—just as no two human beings speak quite alike. The rhythms of the Nurse's speech are quite different from those of Mercutio's explosive outbursts, and these again are totally unlike Benvolio's solemn utterances.

With the central characters, Romeo and Juliet, Shakespeare takes even greater care. Romeo's witty introspection when he is describing his passion for Rosaline sounds very different from the quiet eloquence with which he speaks his love for Juliet; in the balcony scene Shakespeare shows the change in Romeo as the young man hesitates between his former rhetoric ('It is the east, and Juliet is the sun') and his new-found simplicity:

> It is my lady. O, it is my love!
> O that she knew she were!

Romeo seems to grow older—to mature—as the play progresses; and the verse both reflects and expresses the change in his character. Juliet is more straightforward, and the verse she speaks creates a character of purity and passion. After the death of Tybalt she is confused, and her conversation with Lady Capulet shows how she is resolving the confusion: Juliet speaks at the same time to her mother and, with a different meaning, to the audience, who hear her private thoughts.

Such revelations of character can only be made in verse: prose is too inflexible and insensitive. *Romeo and Juliet* needs to be read with great sensitivity—just as one would listen sympathetically to a young girl or boy telling of her/his first love. Don't react to the different styles of writing by dismissing them as false—artificial—unnatural. They are all artificial, in the sense that they are made by art. Occasionally passages of virtuoso writing serve very little purpose: the 'Queen Mab' speech, for instance, tells us something about Mercutio, but it is really intended to be admired—like a firework display. Far more often, however, the form of the verse reveals something about the character who is speaking, or about the situation. The best example of this is the sonnet in *Act 1*, Scene 5, where the most artificial of verse forms is used to express the most natural of emotions—and at the same time to point out the complexity of the situation in which the two young lovers find themselves.

The Elizabethans would have admired the art of *Romeo and Juliet*; today we are more likely to enjoy the play because it seems so real, so true to life as we know it. But a full appreciation must (I believe) combine an understanding of both art and life.

Shakespeare's Verse

Shakespeare's plays are mainly written in 'blank verse', the form preferred by most dramatists in the sixteenth and early seventeenth centuries. It is a very flexible medium, which is capable — like the human speaking voice — of a wide range of tones. Basically the lines, which are unrhymed, are ten syllables long. The syllables have alternating stresses, just like normal English speech; and they divide into five 'feet'. The technical name for this is 'iambic pentameter'.

Tybalt
What, aŕt thou dráwn amońg these héartless hińds?
Túrn thee, Benvólio, loók upoń thy déath.

Benvolio
I dó but keép the peáce. Put uṕ thy swórd,
Or mánage ít to paŕt these meń and mé.

Tybalt
What! Drawń, and tálk of péace? I háte the woŕd,
As Í hate héll, all Mońtagúes, and theé.
Have át thee, cowárd.

1, 1, 63–9

Here the pentameter accommodates a variety of speech tones — Tybalt's angry challenge, Benvolio's steady calm, and the scorn and hatred with which Tybalt renews his attack. In this quotation, most of the lines are regular in length and normal in iambic stress pattern. Sometimes Shakespeare deviates from the norm, varying the stress patterns for unusual emphasis, and writing lines that are longer or shorter than ten syllables. The stress is reversed, for instance, in Tybalt's 'Turn thee', and a threatening movement (rather than words) completes the line after 'coward'.

The speech of Prince Escalus, a little later in this scene, demonstrates another feature of Shakespeare's verse.

Prince

On paín of tórture, fróm those blóody hańds
Throw yoúr misteḿper'd weápons tó the groúnd,
And heár the séntence óf your móved prince.

1, 1, 84–6

Sometimes the grammatical unit of meaning is contained within the verse line — 'And hear the sentence of your moved prince'. This allows for a pause at the end of the line, before a new idea is started. At other times the sense runs on from one line to the next — 'from those bloody hands Throw your mistemper'd weapons to the ground'. This makes for the natural fluidity of speech, avoiding monotony but still maintaining the iambic rhythm.

Date and Text

Romeo and Juliet was probably written between 1594 and 1596. The style links it very closely with other plays (particularly *A Midsummer Night's Dream*) that Shakespeare was writing at this time. It was first published in a quarto of 1597, but this text (Q1) is of very poor quality and seems to have been published without the permission of either the dramatist or the acting company which performed it. Most likely, a manuscript was constructed from memory by one or two actors from the earliest productions; and this was sold to the printers — for cash! But their memories were often faulty, and many speeches were mis-recollected, garbled, or even forgotten altogether.

Two years later, in 1599, another version of the play (Q2) was published; and the title page of this quarto — which is the basis of all modern editions — claimed that the text was 'Newly corrected, augmented, and amended'. Shakespeare's own manuscript was probably available to the printer of Q2, although occasionally — perhaps where the handwriting was illegible — he turned to the printed text of Q1.

Q2 is the basis for the present edition of the play.

Characters in the play

Escalus	*Prince of Verona*
Mercutio	*his kinsman, a friend of Romeo*
The County Paris	*another kinsman, suitor to Juliet*
	('County'=Count)
Montague	*head of a noble family in Verona which has been at enmity with the Capulets for a long time*
Lady Montague	*his wife*
Romeo	*his son*
Benvolio	*his nephew, Romeo's friend*
Abram	
Balthasar	*servants of Montague*
Capulet	*head of a noble family in Verona which is hostile to the Montagues*
Lady Capulet	*his wife*
Juliet	*his daughter*
Cousin Capulet	*his relative*
Tybalt	*Lady Capulet's nephew*
Nurse	*to Juliet*
Peter	
Sampson	*servants of Capulet*
Gregory	
Friar Laurence	
Friar John	*Franciscan friars*
An Apothecary	
Three Musicians	
The Chorus	

Citizens of Verona, masquers, pages, servants, watchmen

Prologue

Enter Chorus

Chorus

Two households, both alike in dignity,
   In fair Verona, where we lay our scene,
From ancient grudge break to new mutiny,
   Where civil blood makes civil hands unclean.
5 From forth the fatal loins of these two foes
   A pair of star-cross'd lovers take their life;
Whose misadventur'd piteous overthrows
   Doth with their death bury their parents' strife.
The fearful passage of their death-mark'd love,
10   And the continuance of their parents' rage,
Which, but their children's end, nought could
remove,
   Is now the two hours' traffic of our stage;
The which if you with patient ears attend,
What here shall miss, our toil shall strive to mend.
                                [*Exit*

Act I

Act I   Scene I

In a public place, the servants of the
house of Capulet quarrel with servants
from the house of Montague. Young
men from the two families join in the
fighting, and even the old men
(Capulet and Montague) try to draw
their swords. The townspeople of
Verona try to separate the enemies, and
the Prince himself commands them to
keep the peace.

When the fighting has stopped,
Montague and his wife question
Benvolio. They want to know who
started the quarrel; and they are also
anxious about their son, Romeo.
Romeo did not join in the fighting.
Benvolio explains that Romeo has been
behaving strangely: he has been
avoiding company for the past few
days. Suddenly Romeo appears. His
parents hurry away, leaving Benvolio
to hear Romeo's explanations for his
strange conduct. Romeo is in love with
a woman; but she does not love
Romeo.

1   *carry coals :* be insulted (a
sixteenth-century slang phrase).

2   *collier :* a man who ⎫
(literally) carries coal. ⎪
3   *choler :* anger ⎬ these three
4   *collar :* i.e. ⎪ words all
the hangman's noose. ⎭ sound alike.

3   *and :* if
draw : draw their swords (i.e.
fight).

4   *while :* as long as.
draw : keep, hold back.

5   When I am angry ('moved') I am
quick to fight.

Scene I *Verona*

> *Enter* Sampson *and* Gregory, *armed with
> swords and bucklers*

Sampson

Gregory, on my word, we'll not carry coals.

Gregory

No, for then we should be colliers.

Sampson

I mean, and we be in choler, we'll draw.

Gregory

Ay, while you live, draw your neck out of the collar.

Sampson

5 I strike quickly, being moved.

Gregory

But thou art not quickly moved to strike.

Sampson

A dog of the house of Montague moves me.

Gregory

To move is to stir, and to be valiant is to stand:
therefore, if thou art moved, thou runnest away.

Sampson

10 A dog of that house shall move me to stand. I will
take the wall of any man or maid of Montague's.

Gregory

That shows thee a weak slave; for the weakest goes
to the wall.

Sampson

'Tis true; and therefore women, being the weaker

6   But you are not easily ('quickly')
made so angry ('moved') that you will
fight (Gregory implies that Sampson is
really a coward).

8   *stand :* i.e. fight.

11   *take the wall :* In an Elizabethan
street, the safest place to walk was close
to the buildings; rubbish was thrown
into the middle of the road.

14–15 *the weaker vessels :* a biblical
expression, meaning 'the weaker sex',
derived from the First Epistle of Peter
(3:7).

15   *thrust to the wall :* pushed aside
(there is a proverb 'The weakest goes
to the wall').

19   *men :* Gregory believes that only
the men, not the women, are involved
in the feud.

20   *'Tis all one :* it makes no
difference.

24   *maidenheads :* virginity.

25   *in what sense :* with what
meaning.

26   *take it in sense :* feel it.

27   *stand :* be erect.

28   *a pretty piece of flesh :* sexually
active.

30   *poor-john :* dried fish (Gregory is
insulting Sampson's virility).
tool : sword.

32   *back :* support.

35   *marry :* by the Virgin Mary (a
mild oath).

36   *take . . . sides :* act legally.

38   *list :* like.

39   *bite my thumb :* make a rude
gesture.

40   *bear :* tolerate.

15 vessels, are ever thrust to the wall. Therefore I will
push Montague's men from the wall, and thrust his
maids to the wall.

Gregory
The quarrel is between our masters, and us their
men.

Sampson
20 'Tis all one. I will show myself a tyrant. When I
have fought with the men, I will be civil with the
maids—I will cut off their heads.

Gregory
The heads of the maids?

Sampson
Ay, the heads of the maids—or their maidenheads.
25 Take it in what sense thou wilt.

Gregory
They must take it in sense that feel it.

Sampson
Me they shall feel while I am able to stand; and 'tis
known I am a pretty piece of flesh.

Gregory
'Tis well thou art not fish; if thou hadst, thou hadst
30 been poor-john. Draw thy tool. Here comes two of
the house of the Montagues.

Enter Abram *and* Balthasar

Sampson
My naked weapon is out. Quarrel. I will back thee.

Gregory
How! Turn thy back and run?

Sampson
Fear me not.

Gregory
35 No, marry! I fear thee!

Sampson
Let us take the law of our sides; let them begin.

Gregory
I will frown as I pass by, and let them take it as they
list.

Sampson
Nay, as they dare. I will bite my thumb at them,
40 which is disgrace to them if they bear it.

Abram
Do you bite your thumb at us, sir?

Sampson
I do bite my thumb, sir.

Abram
Do you bite your thumb at us, sir?

Sampson
[*Aside to* Gregory] Is the law of our side if I say
45 'ay'?

Gregory
[*Aside to Sampson*] No.

Sampson
No, sir, I do not bite my thumb at you, sir. But I
bite my thumb, sir.

Gregory
Do you quarrel, sir?

Abram
50 Quarrel, sir! No, sir.

Sampson
If you do, sir, I am for you. I serve as good a man as
you.

Abram
No better.

Sampson
Well, sir.

Enter Benvolio

Gregory
55 [*Aside to* Sampson] Say, 'better'; here comes one
of my master's kinsmen.

Sampson
Yes, better, sir.

Abram
You lie.

Sampson
Draw, if you be men. Gregory, remember thy
60 swashing blow.

[*They fight*

Benvolio
Part, fools!
Put up your swords; you know not what you do.
[*He beats down their swords*

51   *I am for you :* I will join you.

60   *swashing :* slashing.

62   *put up :* sheathe.

63   *art thou drawn :* is your sword
drawn?
      heartless hinds : (a) servants who
lack courage ('heart'); (b) female deer
without a male leader ('hart').

65   *but :* only.
66   *manage it :* use it properly.
      part : separate

69   *Have at thee :* Tybalt warns
Benvolio that he is about to attack.

70   *bills :* weapons with long handles
and axe-heads.
      partisans : broad-headed spears.

71s.d.   *gown :* dressing-gown

73   *long sword :* heavy, old-fashioned,
sword.

76   *in spite :* in defiance.

80   The Capulets and the Montagues
have used their swords ('steel')
dishonourably (profanely) by fighting
against each other and staining the
swords with the blood of neighbours.

Enter Tybalt

Tybalt
What, art thou drawn among these heartless
  hinds?
Turn thee, Benvolio, look upon thy death.
      Benvolio
65 I do but keep the peace. Put up thy sword,
Or manage it to part these men with me.
      Tybalt
What! Drawn, and talk of peace? I hate the word,
As I hate hell, all Montagues, and thee.
Have at thee, coward!   [*They fight*

Enter several Citizens, *with weapons*

Citizens
70 Clubs, bills, and partisans! Strike! Beat them
down! Down with the Capulets! Down with the
Montagues!

Enter Capulet *in his gown, and* Lady
Capulet

Capulet
What noise is this? Give me my long-sword, ho!
      Lady Capulet
A crutch, a crutch! Why call you for a sword?
      Capulet
75 My sword, I say! Old Montague is come,
And flourishes his blade in spite of me.

Enter Montague *and* Lady Montague

Montague
Thou villain Capulet! Hold me not; let me go.
      Lady Montague
Thou shalt not stir one foot to seek a foe.

Enter Prince Escalus *with* Attendants

Prince
Rebellious subjects, enemies to peace,
80 Profaners of this neighbour-stained steel—
Will they not hear? What ho! You men, you beasts,
That quench the fire of your pernicious rage
With purple fountains issuing from your veins!

84 *On pain of torture :* Escalus threatens to torture the fighters if they do not throw down their weapons.

85 *mistemper'd :* (a) angry; (b) intemperate, improper; (c) badly made (steel is 'tempered' by being hardened so that it becomes tough and resilient).

86 *moved :* angry

87 *bred of an airy word :* caused by some trivial remark.

91 *beseeming :* suitable.

92 *as old :* i.e. as old as the weapons.

93 *canker'd with peace :* rusty because the citizens have been at peace, and are not accustomed to fighting.

canker'd hate : malignant hatred.

95 The penalty for breaking the peace will be death.

99 *know :* learn

our further pleasure : what else I decide to do.

100 *common :* public.

102 *set . . . abroach :* opened up (a cask of liquor or gunpowder is opened by being 'set abroach').

103 *by :* present.

105 *close fighting :* fighting hand to hand.

ere : before.

106 *drew :* drew my sword.

in the instant : at that moment.

107 *prepar'd :* already drawn.

110 *nothing hurt withal :* not injured by Tybalt's flourishes.

112 *on part and part :* some on one side, some on the other.

113 *parted either part :* separated both sides.

115 *Right :* very.

fray : scuffle.

117 *Peer'd forth :* looked out from.

118 *abroad :* out of doors.

119 *sycamore :* a species of tree (related to the fig-tree, and the maple), sometimes associated poetically with hopeless lovers.

On pain of torture, from those bloody hands
85 Throw your mistemper'd weapons to the ground,
And hear the sentence of your moved prince.
Three civil brawls, bred of an airy word,
By thee, old Capulet, and Montague,
Have thrice disturb'd the quiet of our streets,
90 And made Verona's ancient citizens
Cast by their grave beseeming ornaments,
To wield old partisans, in hands as old,
Canker'd with peace, to part your canker'd hate.
If ever you disturb our streets again,
95 Your lives shall pay the forfeit of the peace.
For this time, all the rest depart away.
You, Capulet, shall go along with me;
And, Montague, come you this afternoon
To know our further pleasure in this case,
100 To old Freetown, our common judgment-place.
Once more, on pain of death, all men depart.

[*Exeunt all but* Montague, Lady Montague, *and* Benvolio

Montague
Who set this ancient quarrel new abroach?
Speak, nephew, were you by when it began?
Benvolio
Here were the servants of your adversary
105 And yours, close fighting ere I did approach.
I drew to part them; in the instant came
The fiery Tybalt, with his sword prepar'd,
Which, as he breath'd defiance to my ears,
He swung about his head and cut the winds
110 Who, nothing hurt withal, hiss'd him in scorn.
While we were interchanging thrusts and blows,
Came more and more, and fought on part and part,
Till the prince came, who parted either part.
Lady Montague
O where is Romeo? Saw you him to-day?
115 Right glad I am he was not at this fray.
Benvolio
Madam, an hour before the worshipp'd sun
Peer'd forth the golden window of the east,
A troubled mind drove me to walk abroad
Where underneath the grove of sycamore

120	That grows on the west of this city.
122	*made :* went.
	ware : aware.
123	*covert :* shelter.
124	*measuring :* judging.
	affections : desires.
125	Benvolio's own desire was most of all ('most sought') to be alone (i.e. where other people—'most'—were not to be found).
126	His own company was too much for him.
127	*humour :* mood (in this case, desire for solitude).
128	I was glad to avoid (shun) a man who gladly escaped ('fled') from me.
130	*augmenting :* adding to.
132	*all so soon as :* just as soon as.
134	*curtains :* The typical Elizabethan bed had a roof, supported by posts at each corner, and curtains could be drawn all round the bed.
	Aurora : in Greek mythology, goddess of the dawn.
135	*heavy :* sad.
136	*pens :* shuts.
139	*portentous :* ominous.
142	*of :* from.
143	*importun'd :* asked.

120 (That westward rooteth from this city side)
So early walking did I see your son.
Towards him I made, but he was ware of me,
And stole into the covert of the wood.
I, measuring his affections by my own,
125 Which then most sought where most might not be found,
Being one too many by my weary self,
Pursu'd my humour not pursuing his,
And gladly shunn'd who gladly fled from me.

Montague
Many a morning hath he there been seen,
130 With tears augmenting the fresh morning's dew,
Adding to clouds more clouds with his deep sighs;
But all so soon as the all-cheering sun
Should in the farthest east begin to draw
The shady curtains from Aurora's bed,
135 Away from light steals home my heavy son,
And private in his chamber pens himself,
Shuts up his windows, locks fair daylight out,
And makes himself an artificial night.
Black and portentous must this humour prove
140 Unless good counsel may the cause remove.

Benvolio
My noble uncle, do you know the cause?

Montague
I neither know it nor can learn of him.

Benvolio
Have you importun'd him by any means?

145   *his . . . counsellor :* confiding his
feelings to himself.
147   *close :* mysterious.
148   *sounding :* investigation.
discovery : exploration,
understanding.
149   *envious :* malicious.

153   I would be as glad to cure his
sorrow as to learn what it is.

154   *So please you :* if you please.
155   *his grievance :* what is worrying
(grieving) him.
or be much denied : unless he is
very firm in refusing to answer my
questions.
156   *I would thou wert so happy :* I
hope you will be so lucky.
by thy stay : by staying here.
157   *true shrift :* confession of the
truth.
158   *morrow :* morning.
so young : Romeo has been up
very early, and he is surprised to hear
what time it is.

167   *in his view :* at first sight.
168   *in proof :* in fact, in experience.

Montague
Both by myself and many other friends.
145 But he, his own affections' counsellor,
Is to himself—I will not say how true—
But to himself so secret and so close,
So far from sounding and discovery,
As is the bud bit with an envious worm
150 Ere he can spread his sweet leaves to the air,
Or dedicate his beauty to the sun.
Could we but learn from whence his sorrows grow,
We would as willingly give cure as know.

Enter Romeo.

Benvolio
See where he comes! So please you, step aside;
155 I'll know his grievance, or be much denied.
Montague
I would thou wert so happy by thy stay
To hear true shrift. Come, madam, let's away.
[*Exeunt* Montague *and* Lady Montague
Benvolio
Good morrow, cousin.
Romeo   Is the day so young?
Benvolio
But new struck nine.
Romeo   Ay me! Sad hours seem long.
160 Was that my father that went hence so fast?
Benvolio
It was. What sadness lengthens Romeo's hours?
Romeo
Not having that which, having, makes them short.
Benvolio
In love?
Romeo
Out.
Benvolio
165 Of love?
Romeo
Out of her favour where I am in love.
Benvolio
Alas that love, so gentle in his view,
Should be so tyrannous and rough in proof!

169   *muffled* : blindfolded. Cupid, the god of love in classical mythology, is usually portrayed as a blind boy, with wings, who carries a bow and arrows. He shoots at human beings who, as soon as they are wounded by an arrow, fall passionately in love.

    still : always.

173   The 'hate' referred to is the hatred of the Capulets and Montagues; the 'love' is Romeo's love for his mistress. We learn later that her name is Rosaline; and that she is a Capulet.

174   *brawling* : quarrelling.

175   *of nothing first create* : created out of nothing in the first place.

177   *well-seeming* : apparently beautiful.

179   *Still-waking* : always awake.

180   *that feel no love in this* : have no love in return.

181   *coz* : cousin.

182   *oppression* : heavy burden.

183   This is where love (i.e. Benvolio's love) is at fault.

184–6   *Griefs . . . thine* : Romeo now explains what he means by 'love's transgression'.

185   *propagate* : breed from.
    it : i.e. Romeo's heart.

186   *more* : i.e. griefs (this time, Benvolio's griefs).

189   *purg'd* : purified.

192   *gall* : poison.
    preserving : healing.

193   *Soft* : wait a moment.
    go along : go with you.

194   *And if* : if.

Romeo
Alas that love, whose view is muffled still,
170 Should without eyes see pathways to his will!
Where shall we dine? O me, what fray was here?
Yet tell me not, for I have heard it all.
Here's much to do with hate, but more with love;
Why then, O brawling love! O loving hate!
175 O anything of nothing first create.
O heavy lightness, serious vanity,
Misshapen chaos of well-seeming forms,
Feather of lead, bright smoke, cold fire, sick health,
Still-waking sleep, that is not what it is!
180 This love feel I, that feel no love in this.
Dost thou not laugh?
    Benvolio   No, coz, I rather weep.
    Romeo
Good heart, at what?
    Benvolio
                At thy good heart's oppression.
    Romeo
Why, such is love's transgression.
Griefs of mine own lie heavy in my breast,
185 Which thou wilt propagate, to have it press'd
With more of thine. This love that thou hast shown
Doth add more grief to too much of mine own.
Love is a smoke made with the fume of sighs;
Being purg'd, a fire sparkling in lovers' eyes;
190 Being vex'd, a sea nourish'd with lovers' tears.
What is it else? A madness most discreet,
A choking gall, and a preserving sweet.
Farewell, my coz.   *[Going*
    Benvolio   Soft, I will go along;
And if you leave me so, you do me wrong.
    Romeo
195 Tut, I have lost myself; I am not here;
This is not Romeo, he's some other where.
    Benvolio
Tell me, in sadness, who is that you love.

196 *some other where* : somewhere
else.
197 *in sadness* : seriously.
199 *sadly* : seriously

203 *I aim'd so near* : I was nearly
right.
     suppos'd : guessed.
204 *right good markman* : very good
shot.
     she's fair I love : the woman I
love is beautiful.
205 *a right fair mark* : a very clear
mark (= target).
207 *Cupid's arrow* : see note to line
167.
     Dian : Diana, goddess of chastity
in classical mythology.
     wit : sense, intelligence.
208 *proof* : armour.
209 *uncharm'd* : secure.
210 She will not wait to be besieged
by the affectionate words ('terms') of a
lover.
212 She will not yield her honour for
money (although gold would seduce a
saint). In classical mythology the
princess Danae was locked up in a
tower made of brass—but she was
seduced by Jove, who appeared in a
shower of gold.
213-4 *only . . . store* : she is poor only
that when she dies, her fertility ('store')
perishes with her beauty.
215 *still* : always.
216 *sparing* : economy.
217 *starv'd* : killed.
218 Prevents generations to come
('posterity') from inheriting any
beauty.
219 *fair* : (a) lovely; (b) honest.
220 The lady hopes to win heavenly
happiness ('bliss') by refusing human
love (and this is what makes Romeo
'despair').
221 *forsworn to love* : sworn never to
fall in love.
222 *live dead* : live as if I were dead.
226 Look at other beautiful women.

Romeo
What, shall I groan and tell thee?
    Benvolio
Groan! Why, no; but sadly tell me who.
    Romeo
200 Bid a sick man in sadness make his will.
Ah, word ill urg'd to one that is so ill!
In sadness, cousin, I do love a woman.
    Benvolio
I aim'd so near when I suppos'd you lov'd.
    Romeo
A right good markman! And she's fair I love.
    Benvolio
205 A right fair mark, fair coz, is soonest hit.
    Romeo
Well, in that hit you miss. She'll not be hit
With Cupid's arrow: she hath Dian's wit;
And, in strong proof of chastity well arm'd,
From love's weak childish bow she lives
    uncharm'd.
210 She will not stay the siege of loving terms,
Nor bide th'encounter of assailing eyes,
Nor ope her lap to saint-seducing gold.
O she is rich in beauty; only poor
That, when she dies, with beauty dies her store.
    Benvolio
215 Then she hath sworn that she will still live chaste?
    Romeo
She hath, and in that sparing makes huge waste.
For beauty, starv'd with her severity,
Cuts beauty off from all posterity.
She is too fair, too wise, wisely too fair,
220 To merit bliss by making me despair:
She hath forsworn to love, and in that vow
Do I live dead that live to tell it now.
    Benvolio
Be rul'd by me; forget to think of her.
    Romeo
O teach me how I should forget to think!
    Benvolio
225 By giving liberty unto thine eyes;
Examine other beauties.

227   To make me think ('call in
question') even more about her beauty,
which is exquisite.
228   *happy* : lucky.
    masks. Ladies very often covered
part of their faces with black masks (see
illustration) when they appeared in
public, especially at grand balls such as
the Capulet ball in *Act 1*, Scene 5.
232   *passing fair* : extremely beautiful.
233   *note* : reminder (like a note
written in the margin of a book).
234   *pass'd* : surpassed, excelled.
236   *I'll pay that doctrine* : I'll make you
quite sure that my teaching ('doctrine')
is right.
    die in debt : die in the attempt.

Romeo   'Tis the way
To call hers, exquisite, in question more.
These happy masks that kiss fair ladies' brows,
Being black, puts us in mind they hide the fair;
230 He that is strucken blind cannot forget
The precious treasure of his eyesight lost.
Show me a mistress that is passing fair:
What doth her beauty serve but as a note
Where I may read who pass'd that passing fair?
235 Farewell: thou canst not teach me to forget.
    Benvolio
I'll pay that doctrine, or else die in debt.   [*Exeunt*

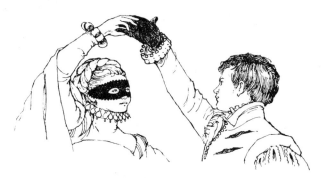

Act 1   Scene 2
The County Paris asks Capulet for
permission to marry his daughter,
Juliet. Capulet is doubtful, because the
girl is very young; but he encourages
Paris to hope for Juliet's love, and
invites him to meet her at the grand
party to be held that night. A servant is
given the list of guests who are also
invited to Capulet's house, but the
servant cannot read. Fortunately,
Romeo and Benvolio are passing, and
the servant asks for Romeo's help.
Romeo reads the list aloud, and
Benvolio has a good idea.

1   *bound* : obliged to keep the
peace.
2   *In penalty alike* : with the same
penalty (punishment) for disobedience.
4   *honourable reckoning* : (a) good
age; (b) good reputation.
5   *at odds* : as enemies.
6   *suit* : request.

Scene 2 *Verona*

Enter Capulet, Paris, *and* Servant
    Capulet
But Montague is bound as well as I,
In penalty alike; and 'tis not hard, I think,
For men so old as we to keep the peace.
    Paris
Of honourable reckoning are you both;
5 And pity 'tis you liv'd at odds so long.
But now, my lord, what say you to my suit?

7	*But :* only.
	saying o'er : repeating.
11	*Ere :* before
	ripe : ready.
12	Girls younger than Juliet have become happy mothers.
13	*marr'd :* spoiled; Capulet echoes an old proverb, 'Soon married, soon marred'.
14	All my children ('hopes') except Juliet have died and been buried.
15	*the hopeful lady of my earth :* Juliet is the only hope of Capulet's life; she is the only child of his body ('earth'); and she has hopes to inherit his estate ('earth').
17	My will (wish) is less important than her agreement.
18	*And she agreed :* once she has agreed.
18–19	*within . . . voice :* my consent and approval ('according voice') will be given where she makes her choice.
20	*old accustom'd :* according to old custom.
22	*store :* number.
25	*Earth-treading stars :* ladies as bright as stars, yet walking on earth.
26	*lusty :* vigorous.
27	*well-apparell'd :* well dressed (i.e. when all the spring flowers are blooming).
28	*limping winter :* winter is slow to leave; spring ('April') is hurrying close behind and treading on his heels.
29	*female buds :* adolescent girls.
30	*Inherit :* possess.
32–3	When you have had a good look at more girls, one of which shall be mine, you may count my daughter among the number, but not have such a high estimation ('reckoning') of her.
37	*stay :* wait.
38–9	*It is written :* one of Shakespeare's contempories, John Lyly, expressed ideas such as these in his novel *Euphues*; but the Servant in this scene is very confused.
39	*meddle :* be busy with.

Capulet
But saying o'er what I have said before:
My child is yet a stranger in the world,
She hath not seen the change of fourteen years;
10 Let two more summers wither in their pride
Ere we may think her ripe to be a bride.
   Paris
Younger than she are happy mothers made.
   Capulet
And too soon marr'd are those so early made.
Earth hath swallow'd all my hopes but she;
15 She is the hopeful lady of my earth.
But woo her, gentle Paris, get her heart,
My will to her consent is but a part;
And she agreed, within her scope of choice
Lies my consent and fair according voice.
20 This night I hold an old accustom'd feast,
Whereto I have invited many a guest
Such as I love; and you, among the store,
One more, most welcome, makes my number more.
At my poor house look to behold this night
25 Earth-treading stars that make dark heaven light.
Such comfort as do lusty young men feel
When well-apparell'd April on the heel
Of limping winter treads—even such delight
Among fresh female buds shall you this night
30 Inherit at my house. Hear all, all see,
And like her most whose merit most shall be:
Which, on more view of many, mine, being one,
May stand in number, though in reckoning none.
Come, go with me. [*To* Servant, *giving him a paper*]
                              Go, sirrah, trudge about
35 Through fair Verona; find those persons out
Whose names are written there, and to them say,
My house and welcome on their pleasure stay.
                              [*Exeunt* Capulet *and* Paris
   Servant
Find them out whose names are written here! It is
written that the shoemaker should meddle with his

40   *yard* : yardstick—a rod used by tailors for measuring lengths of material.

  last : model of the human foot, used for making shoes.

41   *nets* : i.e. for catching fish.

42   *writ* : written.

43   *writing person* : person who did the writing.

44   *learned* : i.e. someone who can read.

  In good time : just at the right time (he sees Romeo and Benvolio— 'the learned'—approaching).

47   *holp* : helped.

48   *cures with* : is cured by.

  languish : suffering.

49   *to thy eye* : if Romeo could see some other girl, he would fall in love afresh.

50   *rank* : foul.

51   *Your . . . that* : Romeo scorns Benvolio's advice, implying that his 'cures' for love are like the traditional 'first-aid' attempts to deal with minor injuries. In Elizabethan times, a bleeding wound could be bandaged with the leaves of the plantain (which in England is a plant growing close to the ground, with broad, flat leaves).

54–6   *a madman* : Romeo describes the way that the Elizabethans treated lunatics; his own sufferings are metaphorical—he is 'in prison' because he is not free to love; his 'food' is the sight of his mistress; he is 'Whipp'd and tormented' by his thoughts.

56   *e'en* : evening (any time, in fact, after twelve noon).

57   *God gi' good e'en* : may God give you a good evening (a more polite form of Romeo's greeting—appropriate from a servant to a gentleman).

58   *mine . . . misery* : I can read my own fate in my unhappiness (perhaps Romeo means that he can see that he was destined to be miserable; or that his misery will be the cause of his death).

40 yard, and the tailor with his last, the fisher with his pencil, and the painter with his nets ; but I am sent to find those persons whose names are here writ, and can never find what names the writing person hath here writ. I must to the learned. In good time !

Enter Benvolio *and* Romeo

Benvolio

45 Tut man, one fire burns out another's burning,
One pain is lessen'd by another's anguish ;
Turn giddy, and be holp by backward turning ;
One desperate grief cures with another's languish.
Take thou some new infection to thy eye,
50 And the rank poison of the old will die.

Romeo

Your plantain leaf is excellent for that.

Benvolio

For what, I pray thee ?

Romeo   For your broken shin.

Benvolio

Why, Romeo, art thou mad ?

Romeo

Not mad, but bound more than a madman is ;
55 Shut up in prison, kept without my food,
Whipp'd and tormented and—good e'en, good fellow.

Servant

God gi' good e'en. I pray, sir, can you read ?

Romeo

Ay, mine own fortune in my misery.

Servant

Perhaps you have learned it without book : but, I
60 pray, can you read any thing you see ?

Romeo

Ay, if I know the letters and the language.

Servant

Ye say honestly ; rest you merry ! [*Turns to go*

59   *without book :* by heart.
62   *rest you merry :* may God keep
you merry (the Servant assumes that
Romeo cannot read).
65   *County :* the count.
67   *Mercutio.* Mercutio is related to
Prince Escalus; perhaps Old Capulet
thinks this connection is more
important than the fact that Mercutio is
one of Montague family.

72   *Up—.* Romeo is impatient, and
will not let the Servant finish his
answer.
80   *crush :* drink.
82   *ancient :* customary.
85   *unattainted :* unprejudiced.
87   *think thy swan a crow.* Swans are
white and beautiful; crows are black
and ugly.

Romeo
Stay, fellow; I can read.   [*He reads the paper*]
  Signor Martino and his wife and daughters;
65 *County Anselme and his beauteous sisters; the lady*
widow of Vitruvio; Signor Placentio, and his lovely
nieces; Mercutio and his brother Valentine; mine
uncle Capulet, his wife and daughters; my fair niece
Rosaline and Livia; Signor Valentio and his cousin
70 *Tybalt; Lucio and the lively Helena.*
A fair assembly: whither should they come?
Servant
Up—
Romeo
Whither? To supper?
Servant
To our house.
Romeo
75 Whose house?
Servant
My master's.
Romeo
Indeed, I should have asked you that before.
Servant
Now I'll tell you without asking. My master is the
great rich Capulet; and if you be not of the house of
80 Montagues, I pray come and crush a cup of wine.
Rest you merry!   [*Exit*
Benvolio
At this same ancient feast of Capulet's
Sups the fair Rosaline, whom thou so loves,
With all the admired beauties of Verona.
85 Go thither; and, with unattainted eye
Compare her face with some that I shall show,
And I will make thee think thy swan a crow.

88–9   When my eyes, which are profoundly religious (their faith is in Rosaline), believe such lies (that other women are as beautiful as Rosaline), may my tears turn into fires.

90   *these*: his eyes (which have often been 'drowned' in tears).

91   *Transparent*: (a) obvious; (b) able to be seen through (like windows: the soul, it was thought, looked through the eyes).

heretics: people with unorthodox religious beliefs; in the sixteenth century such people were often burned to death.

93   *match*: equal.

94   *none else being by*: when no other women were near. Benvolio compares Romeo's eyes to the two pans of a set of scales; the reflection of Rosaline in one eye was balanced ('poised') against the same reflection in the other eye.

96   *crystal*: clear glass.

97   *lady's love*: lady-love, mistress.

99   *scant*: scarcely.

Romeo
When the devout religion of mine eye
Maintains such falsehood, then turn tears to fire!
90 And these who, often drown'd, could never die,
Transparent heretics, be burnt for liars!
One fairer than my love? The all-seeing sun
Ne'er saw her match since first the world begun.
Benvolio
Tut, you saw her fair, none else being by,
95 Herself pois'd with herself in either eye;
But in that crystal scales let there be weigh'd
Your lady's love against some other maid
That I will show you shining at this feast,
And she shall scant show well that now shows best.
Romeo
100 I'll go along, no such sight to be shown,
But to rejoice in splendour of mine own.   [*Exeunt*

Act 1   Scene 3
The Nurse talks about Juliet's childhood, and Lady Capulet tells her daughter that she has a suitor, the County Paris.

2   *by . . . old*. The Nurse swears by the fact that she was a virgin when she was twelve years old.

Scene 3 *Verona: Capulet's house*

Enter Lady Capulet *and* Nurse

Lady Capulet
Nurse, where's my daughter? Call her forth to me.
Nurse
Now, by my maidenhead at twelve year old,

3   *ladybird :* the English 'ladybird' is a minute flying insect, whose wings are red with black spots on them. The Nurse uses the name as a term of endearment.

4   *God forbid :* i.e. that anything has happened to Juliet.

6   *What is your will :* what do you want?

7   *give leave awhile :* leave us for a time.

9   *thou's :* you shall.
counsel : conversation.

10   *of a pretty age :* (a) at an attractive age; (b) old enough.

11   *Faith :* by my faith.

12   *lay :* wager.

13   *teen :* sorrow
be it spoken : it must be said.

15   *Lammas :* Lammas Day is 1 August (the name comes from the Old English word for a loaf of bread, and the festival celebrates the harvest).
tide : time.
odd : a few.

17   *Lammas Eve :* the day before Lammas (i.e. 31 July).

18   *Susan :* the Nurse's own daughter; see Introduction, p. xii.

19   *of an age :* the same age.
with God : i.e. dead.

22   *marry :* by the Virgin Mary.

26   *wormwood :* a bitter herbal preparation (used by the Nurse to persuade the infant to stop suckling and start eating properly).
dug : breast.

27   *dove-house :* doves were housed in round sheds, where they could nest in safety.

29   *bear a brain :* have a good memory.

30   *it :* the baby, Juliet.

32   *tetchy :* irritable.
fall out : quarrel.

I bade her come. What, lamb! What, ladybird!
God forbid! Where's this girl? What Juliet!

Enter Juliet

Juliet
5 How now! Who calls?
Nurse
                    Your mother.
Juliet
Madam, I am here. What is your will?
Lady Capulet
This is the matter. Nurse, give leave awhile;
We must talk in secret—Nurse, come back again.
I have remember'd me, thou's hear our counsel.
10 Thou know'st my daughter's of a pretty age.
Nurse
Faith, I can tell her age unto an hour.
Lady Capulet
She's not fourteen.
Nurse   I'll lay fourteen of my teeth—
And yet, to my teen be it spoken, I have but four—
She's not fourteen. How long is it now
15 To Lammas-tide?
Lady Capulet   A fortnight and odd days.
Nurse
Even or odd, of all days in the year,
Come Lammas Eve at night shall she be fourteen.
Susan and she—God rest all Christian souls!—
Were of an age. Well, Susan is with God;
20 She was too good for me. But, as I said,
On Lammas Eve at night shall she be fourteen.
That shall she, marry! I remember it well.
'Tis since the earthquake now eleven years;
And she was wean'd—I never shall forget it—
25 Of all the days of the year, upon that day.
For I had then laid wormwood to my dug,
Sitting in the sun under the dove-house wall.
My lord and you were then at Mantua—
Nay, I do bear a brain! But, as I said,
30 When it did taste the wormwood on the nipple
Of my dug and felt it bitter, pretty fool,
To see it tetchy and fall out with the dug.

33–4	It seemed to the Nurse as though the dove-house was saying 'Shake' and warning her to go away (because of the earthquake).
	I trow : I am sure.
34	*trudge :* get away.
36	*high-lone :* upright by herself.
	the rood : the cross of Christ.
37	*all about :* everywhere.
38	*broke her brow :* cut her head open.
40	*'A :* he.
41	*took up :* picked up.
	quoth : said.
42	*wit :* sense.
43	*holidom :* holiness.
44	*left :* stopped.
45	*jest :* joke.
	come about : come true.
46	*I warrant :* I'm sure.
	and : if
48	*stinted :* stopped (crying).
49	*hold thy peace :* be quiet.
51	*leave :* stop.
52	*it brow :* its forehead.
53	*stone :* testicle.
56	*com'st to age :* are old enough.
59	*God . . . grace :* may God choose you for His special grace.
60	*nurs'd :* was nurse to: see p. viii
61–2	If I could live to see you married one day, I would have all I could wish for.
65	How do you feel about being married?

'Shake', quoth the dove-house: 'Twas no need, I trow,
To bid me trudge.
35 And since that time it is eleven years;
For then she could stand high-lone; nay, by the rood,
She could have run and waddled all about—
For even the day before she broke her brow,
And then my husband—God be with his soul!
40 'A was a merry man—took up the child:
'Yea', quoth he, 'dost thou fall upon thy face?
Thou wilt fall backward when thou has more wit,
Will thou not, Jule?' And, by my holidom,
The pretty wretch left crying, and said 'Ay'.
45 To see now how a jest shall come about!
I warrant, and I should live a thousand years,
I never should forget it: 'Wilt thou not, Jule?' quoth he,
And, pretty fool, it stinted and said 'Ay'.

Lady Capulet
Enough of this. I pray thee, hold thy peace.

Nurse
50 Yes, madam. Yet I cannot choose but laugh,
To think it should leave crying, and say 'Ay'.
And yet, I warrant, it had upon it brow
A bump as big as a young cockerel's stone,
A perilous knock; and it cried bitterly.
55 'Yea', quoth my husband, 'fall'st upon thy face?
Thou wilt fall backward when thou com'st to age;
Wilt thou not, Jule?' It stinted, and said 'Ay'.

Juliet
And stint thou too, I pray thee Nurse, say I.

Nurse
Peace, I have done. God mark thee to his grace!
60 Thou wast the prettiest babe that e'er I nurs'd:
And I might live to see thee married once,
I have my wish.

Lady Capulet
Marry, that 'marry' is the very theme
I came to talk of. Tell me, daughter Juliet,
65 How stands your disposition to be married?

Juliet
It is an honour that I dream not of.
Nurse
An honour! Were not I thine only nurse,
I would say thou hadst suck'd wisdom from thy
    teat.
Lady Capulet
Well, think of marriage now. Younger than you,
70 Here in Verona, ladies of esteem,
Are made already mothers. By my count,
I was your mother much upon these years
That you are now a maid. Thus then in brief,
The valiant Paris seeks you for his love.
Nurse
75 A man, young lady! Lady, such a man
As all the world—why, he's a man of wax.
Lady Capulet
Verona's summer hath not such a flower.
Nurse
Nay, he's a flower; in faith, a very flower.
Lady Capulet
What say you? Can you love the gentleman?
80 This night you shall behold him at our feast.
Read o'er the volume of young Paris' face
And find delight writ there with beauty's pen.
Examine every married lineament,
And see how one another lends content.

67   *Were . . . nurse :* if I were not the only nurse who has fed you.

70   *ladies of esteem :* noble ladies.
71   *count :* reckoning.
72   *much upon these years :* at just about the same age.

76   *a man of wax :* a perfect model of a man.

78   *in faith :* indeed.

81–92   *Read . . . story.* Lady Capulet makes a long and complicated comparison; she describes Paris as though he were a book.
81   *volume :* part of a book (as the face is part of the whole man).
82   *writ :* written.
83   *married :* harmoniously united.
    lineament : line (in a book); feature (in the face).
84   *one another lends :* one lends to another.
    content : meaning (in a book); beauty (in Paris's face).

85–6 Difficulties in the main text of a book were explained by notes in the margin ('margent'). Lady Capulet tells Juliet that if she finds anything difficult (obscure) in Paris's face, she will be able to understand the expression in his eyes.

87 *unbound :* without a cover (the book); unmarried (the man).

89–90 People like to have good books bound in handsome covers: the lovely outside appearance conceals the excellent contents. In the same way, fish (which are beautiful) are at home, and live happily, in the sea (which is also very beautiful).

91 *in many's eyes :* in the opinion of many people.

92 *gold clasps :* very grand books were fastened with gold clasps, which could even be locked with small keys.

94 By marrying Paris, Juliet will increase her status, not lower it.

95 *grow :* (a) achieve status; (b) become pregnant.

96 *like of :* approve of.

97 *I'll . . . like :* I will look at him with the intention of liking him.
if looking liking move : if looking at Paris is enough to make me like him.

98–9 I will not go any further than you allow me to do.

98 *endart.* The Elizabethans believed that beams of light came from the eyes (like modern electric torch beams), and illuminated the object that was being observed.

99 *fly.* Juliet thinks of her eye-beam as a dart, given power to fly by her mother's approval of Paris.

102 *in extremity :* in a terrible mess.

103 *to wait :* to serve food and drink.
straight : immediately.

104 *the County stays :* Count Paris is waiting for you.

85 And what obscur'd in this fair volume lies
Find written in the margent of his eyes.
This precious book of love, this unbound lover,
To beautify him, only lacks a cover.
The fish lives in the sea, and 'tis much pride
90 For fair without the fair within to hide:
That book in many's eyes doth share the glory,
That in gold clasps locks in the golden story.
So shall you share all that he doth possess,
By having him, making yourself no less.
        Nurse
95 No less? Nay bigger! Women grow by men.
        Lady Capulet
Speak briefly, can you like of Paris' love?
        Juliet
I'll look to like, if looking liking move.
But no more deep will I endart mine eye
Than your consent gives strength to make it fly.

Enter a Servant

        Servant
100 Madam, the guests are come, supper served up,
you called, my young lady asked for, the Nurse
cursed in the pantry, and everything in extremity. I
must hence to wait. I beseech you, follow straight.
        Lady Capulet
We follow thee. [*Exit* Servant] Juliet, the County
stays.
        Nurse
105 Go, girl, seek happy nights to happy days. [*Exeunt*

Act 1   Scene 4

Benvolio and Mercutio are ready to go
to Capulet's party; they will be
accompanied by torch-bearers, and they
will wear masks to avoid identification.
Romeo is not happy—but Mercutio
teases him until he finally agrees to go
with his friends.

1–2   Shall we make a speech, excusing
ourselves (because they have arrived
without invitation), or shall we go in
without any apology?

1   *spoke* : spoken.

2   *shall we on* : shall we go on?

3   Such long-windedness
('prolixity') is old-fashioned (out of
date).

4–6   A party of revellers could have a
leader, who wore fancy-dress, to
announce their arrival.

4   *Cupid* : see note to *1, 1, 169* (and
illustration).

5   *Tartar* : the Tartars, from central
Asia, were famous for shooting with
bow and arrows.
  lath : wood.

6   *crow-keeper* : scarecrow.

7–8   Benvolio now talks as though he
were an actor.

7   *without-book prologue* : address to
the audience (as at the beginning of
Romeo and Juliet), spoken without a
book (i.e. from memory).
  faintly : in a low voice.

8   *the prompter* : it is the prompter's
job to remind actors of the lines they
have forgotten (which they then repeat
after him).

9   *measure* : judge.

10   *measure them a measure* : perform
the steps of a stately dance for them.

11   *for this ambling* : in favour of this
dancing.

12   *heavy* : sad.

16   *stakes* : fixes.

18   *above a common bound* : out of the
ordinary way.

19   *sore* : painfully.
  empierced : pierced through
  shaft : arrow.

21   *bound a pitch* : soar to a height.

Scene 4 *Verona*

Enter Romeo, Mercutio, Benvolio *with
five or six* Masquers and Torchbearers

Romeo
What, shall this speech be spoke for our excuse?
Or shall we on without apology?

Benvolio
The date is out of such prolixity.
We'll have no Cupid hoodwink'd with a scarf,
5 Bearing a Tartar's painted bow of lath,
Scaring the ladies like a crow-keeper;
Nor no without-book prologue, faintly spoke
After the prompter, for our entrance:
But let them measure us by what they will,
10 We'll measure them a measure, and be gone.

Romeo
Give me a torch. I am not for this ambling:
Being but heavy, I will bear the light.

Mercutio
Nay, gentle Romeo, we must have you dance.

Romeo
Not I, believe me: you have dancing shoes
15 With nimble soles; I have a soul of lead
So stakes me to the ground I cannot move.

Mercutio
You are a lover; borrow Cupid's wings,
And soar with them above a common bound.

Romeo
I am too sore empierced with his shaft
20 To soar with his light feathers; and so bound
I cannot bound a pitch above dull woe:
Under love's heavy burden do I sink.

23   If you cannot rise to the
occasion, you will be a burden on love.

29   *case :* cover, mask.
        visage : face.

30   An ugly mask for an ugly face.

31   *curious :* inquisitive.
        quote : observe.

32   *beetle-brows :* heavy, overhanging
eyebrows.
        blush : the mask is (probably)
bright red or pink.

34   *betake him to his legs :* start
dancing.

36   *rushes :* grass and leaves spread
over the floor (as a carpet); they are
'senseless' because they do not feel the
feet of the dancers.

37   *I am proverb'd :* I follow the
advice of the proverb.
        The proverb is 'A good candle-
holder proves a good gamester': the
man who carries the torch (or candle)
does not take part in the gambling-
game himself—and therefore he knows
more about the game than those who
are personally involved in it.
        grandsire : old-fashioned (as used
by grandparents).

39   *ne'er so fair :* never so good:
gamblers are advised to stop playing
when the game seems to be at its best.
        done : finished.

40   *dun :* dark brown. Mercutio puns
on Romeo's word 'done', saying that
only a mouse should be dark and quiet.
Perhaps 'dun' is 'the constable's own
word' because the police should be
silent and inconspicuous when hunting
a criminal.

41   *draw thee from the mire :* pull you
out of the mud; 'Dun' was a common
name for a horse—and horses
frequently got stuck in the mud
because the roads were unsurfaced.
There was a Christmas game called
'Dun-in-the-mire', in which the
players pulled a log (representing Dun
the Horse) out of imaginary mud.

Mercutio
And, to sink in it, should you burden love;
Too great oppression for a tender thing.
    Romeo
25 Is love a tender thing? It is too rough,
    Too rude, too boisterous; and it pricks like thorn.
    Mercutio
If love be rough with you, be rough with love:
Prick love for pricking, and you beat love down.
Give me a case to put my visage in.
                        [*He puts on a mask*
30 A visor for a visor! What care I
What curious eye doth quote deformities?
Here are the beetle-brows shall blush for me.

    Benvolio
Come, knock and enter; and no sooner in,
But every man betake him to his legs.
    Romeo
35 A torch for me! Let wantons light of heart
    Tickle the senseless rushes with their heels,
    For I am proverb'd with a grandsire phrase:
    I'll be a candle-holder, and look on.
    The game was ne'er so fair, and I am done.
    Mercutio
40 Tut, dun's the mouse, the constable's own word!
    If thou art dun, we'll draw thee from the mire,

42 *save your reverence*. Mercutio makes a mock-apology because he has almost used an obscene word, and he is comparing Romeo's love to filthy mud.

43 *burn daylight :* waste time.

44 *that's not so :* Romeo pretends to misunderstand Mercutio's meaning.

46 *Take our good meaning :* take the words with the meaning I intended.
judgement : good sense.

47 *in that :* i.e. in our intentions.
ere : rather.
five wits : the five senses (sight, hearing, smell, taste, and touch).

48 *mean well :* have good intentions.
masque : party.

49 *wit :* sense.

53 *Queen Mab.* This fantastic personage is the creation of Shakespeare's imagination (there is no such creature in fairy-tales written before this play).

54 *midwife :* nurse who assists with the birth of a baby; Queen Mab is responsible for bringing dreams to life.

55–6 *In shape . . . alderman.* Shakespeare is thinking of the large ring worn by an influential citizen ('alderman'); the stone would be agate, because this can easily be carved into some shape suitable for stamping on wax when sealing a document.

57 *atomi :* atoms, tiny creatures.

60 *joiner :* carpenter; squirrels have sharp teeth, and gnaw through wood.
grub : a worm that bores holes inside nuts.

61 *Time out o'mind :* from time immemorial.

62 *waggon-spokes :* the spokes of the wheels.
spinners : spiders.

63 *cover :* canopy, hood.

64 *traces :* harness.

Or—save your reverence—love, wherein thou stick'st
Up to the ears. Come, we burn daylight, ho!
    Romeo
Nay, that's not so.
    Mercutio   I mean, sir, in delay
45 We waste our lights in vain, like lamps by day.
Take our good meaning, for our judgement sits
Five times in that ere once in our five wits.
    Romeo
And we mean well in going to this masque;
But 'tis no wit to go.
    Mercutio   Why, may one ask?
    Romeo
50 I dream'd a dream tonight.
    Mercutio   And so did I.
    Romeo
Well, what was yours?
    Mercutio   That dreamers often lie.
    Romeo
In bed asleep, while they do dream things true.
    Mercutio
O, then I see Queen Mab hath been with you.
She is the fairies' midwife, and she comes
55 In shape no bigger than an agate stone
On the fore-finger of an alderman,
Drawn with a team of little atomi
Over men's noses as they lie asleep.
Her chariot is an empty hazelnut
60 Made by the joiner squirrel or old grub,
Time out o' mind the fairies' coachmakers.
Her waggon-spokes made of long spinners' legs;
The cover of the wings of grasshoppers;
Her traces, of the smallest spider web;

65 *collars* : A horse pulling a waggon wears a collar round its neck; but Shakespeare seems to be thinking also of the shafts of the waggon, which could appropriately (in this case) be made of moonbeams.

66 *film* : gossamer (the thread with which spiders make their webs).

68–9 Elizabethans said (not seriously) that tiny worms were bred in the fingers of lazy maid-servants.

70 *state* : splendour.

72 *curtsies* : bending the knee as a sign of respect; courtesy.

73 *straight* : immediately.

78 *smelling out a suit* : finding someone who will pay him to present a case at court.

79 *tithe-pig* : Every tenth pig born in a parish was given to the parson of that parish; the parson's salary was a 'tithe' (= tenth) that of the total income of the parish.

80 *'a* : he.

81 *benifice* : church appointment.

84 *breaches* : holes made in defence walls (through which he can attack the enemy).
ambuscados : ambushes.
Spanish blades : The best swords were made in Toledo, in Spain.

85 *healths . . . deep* : very heavy drinking.
anon : at once.

86 *starts* : is startled.

88 *very* : same.

89 *plaits the manes* : makes the manes knotted and untidy.

90 *elf-locks* : elves (small fairies) were responsible for making the hair ('locks') untidy, in order to punish lazy girls. Queen Mab makes the knots and tangles even more difficult to comb out when she 'bakes' them.

91 *bodes* : will follow.

92 *hag* : witch.

93 *learns* : teaches.
bear : (a) bear weight on their bodies; (b) bear children.

94 *carriage* : posture.

98 *vain* : empty.

65 Her collars, of the moonshine's watery beams;
Her whip, of cricket's bone; the lash, of film;
Her waggoner, a small grey-coated gnat,
Not half so big as a round little worm
Prick'd from the lazy finger of a maid;
70 And in this state she gallops night by night
Through lovers' brains, and then they dream of love;
O'er courtiers' knees, that dream on curtsies straight;
O'er lawyers' fingers, who straight dream on fees;
O'er ladies' lips, who straight on kisses dream—
75 Which oft the angry Mab with blisters plagues,
Because their breaths with sweetmeats tainted are.
Sometime she gallops o'er a courtier's nose,
And then dreams he of smelling out a suit;
And sometime comes she with a tithe-pig's tail,
80 Tickling the parson's nose as 'a lies asleep,
Then dreams he of another benefice.
Sometime she driveth o'er a soldier's neck
And then dreams he of cutting foreign throats,
Of breaches, ambuscados, Spanish blades,
85 Of healths five fathom deep; and then anon
Drums in his ear, at which he starts and wakes,
And being thus frighted, swears a prayer or two,
And sleeps again. This is that very Mab
That plaits the manes of horses in the night,
90 And bakes the elf-locks in foul sluttish hairs,
Which once untangled much misfortune bodes;
This is the hag, when maids lie on their backs,
That presses them, and learns them how to bear—
Making them women of good carriage.
95 This is she—
Romeo   Peace, peace, Mercutio, peace!
Thou talk'st of nothing.
Mercutio   True, I talk of dreams,
Which are the children of an idle brain,
Begot of nothing but vain fantasy;
Which is as thin of substance as the air,
100 And more inconstant than the wind, who woos

101   *Even now :* at one moment.
          bosom : heart.
102   *anger'd :* i.e. because the frozen
          north remains cold.
104   *from ourselves :* from our real
          purpose.

106   *misgives :* warns.
107   *yet hanging in the stars :* ordained
          in the stars, but not yet revealed.
109   *expire :* put an end to.
          term : period.
110   *clos'd :* enclosed.
111   *forfeit :* payment.
          untimely : early.
112   *steerage :* direction, responsibility
          for steering.
113   *sail :* which way I sail.
114   *Strike, drum :* Benvolio speaks to
          the drummer who is leading the group
          of revellers.

Act 1   Scene 5
At Capulet's feast, Romeo sees Juliet
for the first time and immediately falls
in love with her. Tybalt, Juliet's
cousin, is angry when he recognizes
Romeo ; he wants to fight, but Old
Capulet restrains his nephew. Romeo
and Juliet speak to each other. As the
guests are leaving the Capulet house,
Juliet questions her Nurse about the
identity of the unknown young man
who was so attractive. She confesses (to
herself and to the audience) that she
has fallen in love with him.

s.d.   *Masquers.* See p. xiii

1   *take away :* remove the dishes.
2   *trencher :* plate.
5   *joint-stools :* stools made by a
      carpenter.

Even now the frozen bosom of the north,
And, being anger'd, puffs away from thence,
Turning his face to the dew-dropping south.
Benvolio
This wind you talk of blows us from ourselves ;
105 Supper is done, and we shall come too late.
Romeo
I fear too early ; for my mind misgives
Some consequence yet hanging in the stars
Shall bitterly begin his fearful date
With this night's revels, and expire the term
110 Of a despised life clos'd in my breast
By some vile forfeit of untimely death.
But He that hath the steerage of my course
Direct my sail ! On, lusty gentlemen.
Benvolio
Strike, drum.   [*Exeunt*

Scene 5 *Verona : Capulet's house*

> *Servants* hurry about the stage ; enter
> Romeo, Mercutio, Benvolio *with the*
> *other* Masquers *and* Torchbearers

        1 Servant
Where's Potpan, that he helps not to take away ? He
shift a trencher ! He scrape a trencher !
        2 Servant
When good manners shall lie all in one or two men's
hands, and they unwashed too, 'tis a foul thing.
        1 Servant
5 Away with the joint-stools ; remove the court-

5–6   *court-cupboard :* sideboard,
holding silver, linen, fruit and wines
for the banquet.

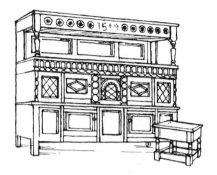

6   *look to the plate :* keep an eye on
the silver.
Good thou : be a góod chap.
7   *marchpane :* marzipan.
as : if.
7–8   *let the porter :* tell the porter.
12   *Great Chamber :* main hall.
14   *the longer liver :* the one who lives
longest.
17   *walk a bout :* have a dance.
19   *deny :* refuse.
makes dainty : makes a fuss.
20   *am I come near ye :* have I
guessed the truth about you?
22   *visor :* mask.

26   *A hall :* make room.
foot it : get on with the dancing.
27   *turn the tables up :* put the tables
on top on each other (to make more
room for the dancing).
28   *quench :* put out.
29   *unlook'd-for :* unexpected; he
refers to the arrival of the masquers.

cupboard; look to the plate. Good thou, save me a
piece of marchpane; and, as thou loves me, let the
porter let in Susan Grindstone and Nell.
                                    [*Exit* 2 Servant
Antony! And Potpan!

Enter 3 *and* 4 Servants
    3 Servant
10 Ay, boy; ready.
    1 Servant
You are looked for and called for, asked for and
sought for, in the Great Chamber.
    4 Servant
We cannot be here and there too.
    1 Servant
Cheerly, boys; be brisk awhile, and the longer liver
15 take all.   [*Exeunt* 3 *and* 4 Servants

        Enter Capulet, Lady Capulet, Juliet,
        Tybalt, Nurse *and other guests, meeting
        the* Masquers
    Capulet
Welcome, gentlemen! Ladies that have their toes
Unplagu'd with corns will walk a bout with you.
Ah my mistresses, which of you all
Will now deny to dance? She that makes dainty,
20 She, I'll swear, hath corns; am I come near ye now?
Welcome, gentlemen! I have seen the day
That I have worn a visor, and could tell
A whispering tale in a fair lady's ear
Such as would please. 'Tis gone, 'tis gone, 'tis gone.
25 You are welcome, gentlemen! Come, musicians
    play.   [*Music plays, and they dance.*
A hall! a hall! give room, and foot it, girls!
More light, you knaves! and turn the tables up,
And quench the fire, the room is grown too hot.
Ah, sirrah, this unlook'd-for sport comes well.
30 Nay, sit, nay, sit, good cousin Capulet,
For you and I are past our dancing days;
How long is 't now since last yourself and I
Were in a masque?

33	*By'r Lady :* by Our Lady (the Virgin Mary).
35	*nuptial :* wedding.
36	*Pentecost :* Whitsuntide.
39	*Will you tell me that :* don't tell me that.
40	*but :* only.
	a ward : a minor (under the age of 21).
41	*enrich the hand :* make the hand richer (i.e. by holding it).
45	*Ethiop :* black man.
46	Beauty like that is too good for everyday use, and too valuable for this earth.
47	*shows :* appears.
49	*The measure done :* when this dance is ended.
	place of stand : where she stands.
50	*rude :* rough.
51	*Forswear :* deny.
55	*antic :* comic (i.e. the mask that Romeo is wearing).
56	*fleer :* sneer.
	solemnity : ceremony.
57	*stock and honour :* honourable breeding.
	kin : family.
58	*hold :* consider.
61	*spite :* contempt.

Second Capulet

                By'r Lady, thirty years.

Capulet

What, man! 'Tis not so much, 'tis not so much:

35 'Tis since the nuptial of Lucentio,

Come Pentecost as quickly as it will,

Some five and twenty years; and then we masqu'd.

Second Capulet

'Tis more, 'tis more; his son is elder, sir.

His son is thirty.

Capulet   Will you tell me that?

40 His son was but a ward two years ago.

Romeo

What lady 's that which doth enrich the hand

Of yonder knight?

1 Servant

I know not, sir.

Romeo

O, she doth teach the torches to burn bright!

It seems she hangs upon the cheek of night

45 As a rich jewel in an Ethiop's ear:

Beauty too rich for use, for earth too dear!

So shows a snowy dove trooping with crows,

As yonder lady o'er her fellows shows.

The measure done, I'll watch her place of stand,

50 And, touching hers, make blessed my rude hand.

Did my heart love till now? Forswear it, sight!

For I ne'er saw true beauty till this night.

Tybalt

This, by his voice, should be a Montague.

Fetch me my rapier, boy. What, dares the slave

55 Come hither, cover'd with an antic face,

To fleer and scorn at our solemnity?

Now, by the stock and honour of my kin,

To strike him dead I hold it not a sin.

Capulet

Why, how now, kinsman! Wherefore storm you so?

Tybalt

60 Uncle, this is a Montague, our foe.

A villain that is hither come in spite

To scorn at our solemnity this night.

Capulet

Young Romeo, is it?

Tybalt   'Tis he, that villain Romeo.

Capulet

Content thee, gentle coz, let him alone;

65 'A bears him like a portly gentleman.

And, to say truth, Verona brags of him

To be a virtuous and well-govern'd youth.

I would not for the wealth of all this town

Here in my house do him disparagement;

70 Therefore be patient, take no note of him.

It is my will, the which if thou respect,

Show a fair presence and put off these frowns,

An ill-beseeming semblance for a feast.

Tybalt

It fits when such a villain is a guest;

75 I'll not endure him.

Capulet   He shall be endur'd.

What, goodman boy! I say he shall. Go to!

Am I the master here, or you? Go to!

You'll not endure him! God shall mend my soul!

You'll make a mutiny among my guests.

80 You will set cock-a-hoop! you'll be the man!

Tybalt

Why, uncle, 'tis a shame.

Capulet   Go to, go to;

You are a saucy boy—is 't so indeed?

This trick may chance to scathe you. I know what:

You must contrary me! Marry, 'tis time—

85 Well said, my hearts!—You are a princox, go:

Be quiet, or—More light, more light!—For shame!

I'll make you quiet. What, cheerly, my hearts!

Tybalt

Patience perforce with wilful choler meeting

Makes my flesh tremble in their different greeting.

90 I will withdraw; but this intrusion shall

Now seeming sweet convert to bitterest gall.

[*Exit*

Romeo

If I profane with my unworthiest hand

This holy shrine, the gentle sin is this:

My lips, two blushing pilgrims, ready stand

95 To smooth that rough touch with a tender
kiss.

---

64 *Content thee :* calm yourself.
coz : cousin; the term was used affectionately to refer to *any* relative.
65 *portly :* dignified.
66 *to say truth :* indeed.
brags of : boasts about.
67 *well-govern'd :* good-mannered.
69 *do him disparagement :* dishonour him.
70 *note :* notice.
72 *Show a fair presence :* behave in a friendly manner.
73 *ill-beseeming semblance :* unsuitable appearance.

76 *goodman boy :* unmannerly child.
Go to : shame on you (an expression of impatience).

79 *make a mutiny :* start a fight.
80 *set cock-a-hoop :* cause disorder.
be the man : i.e. give the orders.

81 *shame :* dishonour.

83 *chance :* perhaps.
scathe : injure.
84 *contrary :* contradict.
84–7 *Marry . . . hearts :* Capulet speaks to his guests, and then, (privately) to Tybalt.
85 *princox :* insolent young man.
88 Patience that is forced upon me mixes with the anger ('choler') that I feel of my own free will (wilfully).
89 *my flesh :* my whole body.
different : hostile (i.e. the patience and the anger are hostile to each other).
90 *withdraw :* leave the room.
91 *gall :* poison.

93 *This holy shrine :* i.e. Juliet's hand.

97   Your hand shows proper respect in what it does (i.e. in touching Juliet's hand).

99   *palmers* : pilgrims to Jerusalem who brought back palm leaves to show where they had been.

103   *grant* : i.e. grant my prayer.

104   *Saints* : i.e. statues of saints.

105   *effect* : result (i.e. a kiss).

108   *urg'd* : argued.
109   *by the book* : expertly (as though he had studied the subject in a book).

111   *Marry* : by the Virgin Mary.
       bachelor : young gentleman.

114   *withal* : with.

116   *the chinks* : plenty of money.
117   *My . . . debt* : I owe my life to my enemy.

118   *sport is at the best* : see *1, 4, 39*.

Juliet
Good pilgrim, you do wrong your hand too much,
    Which mannerly devotion shows in this;
For saints have hands that pilgrims' hands do touch,
    And palm to palm is holy palmers' kiss.
Romeo
100 Have not saints lips, and holy palmers too?
Juliet
Ay, pilgrim, lips that they must use in prayer.
Romeo
O then, dear saint, let lips do what hands do!
    They pray: grant thou, lest faith turn to despair.
Juliet
Saints do not move, though grant for prayers' sake.
Romeo
105 Then move not, while my prayers' effect I take.
                                [*He kisses her*
    Thus from my lips, by thine, my sin is purg'd.
Juliet
Then have my lips the sin that they have took.
Romeo
Sin from my lips? O trespass sweetly urg'd!
    Give me my sin again.
Juliet   You kiss by the book.
Nurse
110 Madam, your mother craves a word with you.
                          [Juliet *goes to* Lady Capulet
Romeo
What is her mother?
Nurse   Marry, bachelor,
    Her mother is the lady of the house,
    And a good lady, and a wise, and virtuous.
    I nurs'd her daughter, that you talk'd withal;
115 I tell you, he that can lay hold of her
    Shall have the chinks.
Romeo   Is she a Capulet?
O dear account! My life is my foe's debt.
Benvolio
Away, be gone; the sport is at the best.

Romeo
Ay, so I fear. The more is my unrest.
Capulet
120 Nay, gentlemen, prepare not to be gone;
We have a trifling foolish banquet towards.
[*They whisper to him*
Is it e'en so? Why then, I thank you all;
I thank you, honest gentlemen; good-night.
More torches here! Come on then, let's to bed.
125 Ah, sirrah, by my fay, it waxes late;
I'll to my rest.   [*Exeunt all except* Juliet *and* Nurse
Juliet
Come hither, Nurse. What is yond gentleman?
Nurse
The son and heir of old Tiberio.
Juliet
What's he that now is going out of door?
Nurse
130 Marry, that, I think, be young Petruchio.
Juliet
What's he, that follows there, that would not
dance?
Nurse
I know not.
Juliet
Go, ask his name.—If he be married,
My grave is like to be my wedding-bed.
Nurse
135 His name is Romeo, and a Montague;
The only son of your great enemy.
Juliet
My only love sprung from my only hate!
Too early seen unknown, and known too late!
Prodigious birth of love it is to me,
140 That I must love a loathed enemy.
Nurse
What's this, what's this?
Juliet   A rhyme I learn'd even now
Of one I danc'd withal.
[*One calls within:* 'Juliet!'
Nurse   Anon, anon!
Come, let's away; the strangers all are gone.
[*Exeunt*

121   *foolish :* simple.
      banquet : supper (fruits, sweets
   and wine).
      towards : about to be served.
122   *e'en :* indeed.

125   *fay :* faith.
      waxes : grows.

126   *yond :* yonder.

134   I will die if I can't marry him.
      like : likely.

139   *Prodigious :* ominous, foretelling
   evil.

141   *even :* just.

142s.d.   *within :* from offstage.
142   *Anon :* I'm coming.

Act 2

Chorus

The second speech of the Chorus is only necessary to indicate the passing of time and the change of place. We are told what we already know—that Romeo's love for Rosaline has been forgotten, and that he is now in love with Juliet; and we are given a hint about the difficulties that the lovers will encounter.

2   *gapes* : longs.
      to be his heir : to take his place.
6   *Alike* : i.e. both Romeo and Juliet.
7   *foe suppos'd* : the one who is regarded as his enemy.
      complain : plead for love.
8   *fearful* : terrifying.
9   *held* : considered to be.
10   *breathe* : speak.
      use : are accustomed to.
14   *Tempering* : softening.
      extremity : severity.

Enter Chorus

Chorus

Now old desire doth in his death-bed lie,
   And young affection gapes to be his heir;
That fair for which love groan'd for and would die,
   With tender Juliet match'd, is now not fair.
5 Now Romeo is belov'd and loves again,
   Alike bewitched by the charm of looks.
But to his foe suppos'd he must complain,
   And she steal love's sweet bait from fearful hooks.
Being held a foe, he may not have access
10   To breathe such vows as lovers use to swear;
And she as much in love, her means much less
   To meet her new beloved anywhere.
But passion lends them power, time means, to meet,
Tempering extremity with extreme sweet.   [*Exit*

Act 2   Scene 1

Romeo hides from his friends, and listens to their jokes about his love.

2   *earth* : Romeo addresses his body.
      centre : heart (which he has given to Juliet).

Scene 1 *Verona : outside Capulet's orchard*

Enter Romeo

Romeo

Can I go forward when my heart is here?
Turn back, dull earth, and find thy centre out.

Enter Benvolio *and* Mercutio; Romeo *stands back*

Benvolio

Romeo! My cousin Romeo! Romeo!

4   *stol'n him :* gone secretly.

6   *conjure :* invoke—as a magician invokes the spirits of the dead.

7   The first stage in a magical incantation was the recitation of the different names of the person invoked.

8   *likeness :* shape; it was necessary to specify the form that the disembodied spirit should take when it responded to the conjuror.

9   *satisfied :* i.e. convinced of his identity.

10   *but :* only.

       'love' and 'dove' : typical rhymes of foolish love-poetry.

11   *gossip :* old woman.

       Venus : the classical goddess of love, mother of Cupid.

12   *purblind :* completely blind.

13   *Abraham :* Mercutio compares Cupid with the 'abraham men'—beggars and thieves who, like Cupid, (see illustration, p. 10) were half-naked.

       trim : neatly.

14   *King Cophetua :* the hero of a popular ballad; he fell in love with a humble peasant girl, and married her.

16   *ape :* fool.

       conjure him : raise him up.

20   *demesnes :* territories.

21   *thy likeness :* i.e. in your own person.

22   *And if :* if.

24   *raise :* call up.

       circle : the magic area (in conjuring).

26   *laid it :* satisfied it.

       conjur'd it down : dismissed it.

27   *spite :* injury.

31   *consorted :* associated.

       humorous : damp and moody.

32   *befits :* suits.

33   *hit the mark :* achieve its aim.

Mercutio   He is wise,
And, on my life, hath stol'n him home to bed.
Benvolio
5 He ran this way, and leap'd this orchard wall.
Call, good Mercutio.
Mercutio   Nay, I'll conjure too.
Romeo! Humours! Madman! Passion! Lover!
Appear thou in the likeness of a sigh:
Speak but one rhyme and I am satisfied;
10 Cry but 'Ay me!' Pronounce but 'love' and 'dove';
Speak to my gossip Venus one fair word,
One nickname for her purblind son and heir,
Young Abraham Cupid, he that shot so trim
When King Cophetua lov'd the beggar-maid.
15 He heareth not, he stirreth not, he moveth not:
The ape is dead, and I must conjure him.
I conjure thee by Rosaline's bright eyes,
By her high forehead, and her scarlet lip,
By her fine foot, straight leg, and quivering thigh,
20 And the demesnes that there adjacent lie,
That in thy likeness thou appear to us!
Benvolio
And if he hear thee, thou wilt anger him.
Mercutio
This cannot anger him. 'Twould anger him
To raise a spirit in his mistress' circle
25 Of some strange nature, letting it there stand
Till she had laid it, and conjur'd it down;
That were some spite. My invocation
Is fair and honest: in his mistress' name
I conjure only but to raise up him.
Benvolio
30 Come, he hath hid himself among these trees,
To be consorted with the humorous night:
Blind is his love and best befits the dark.
Mercutio
If love be blind, love cannot hit the mark.

34   *medlar* : a small round fruit, not
ripe for eating until almost rotten and
ready to burst open with juice; because
of this, the medlar was called an 'open
arse' by country people or (as Mercutio
tells us) young girls, 'when they laugh
alone'.

36   *laugh alone* : tell jokes together
(thinking they are not overheard by
adults).

38   *etcetera* : Shakespeare gives scope
for the audience's imagination.
      poperin : a variety of pear named
after the Belgium town of Poperinghe.

39   *truckle-bed* : bed with wheels
instead of legs.

40   *field-bed* : bed in the open air.

Now will he sit under a medlar tree,
35 And wish his mistress were that kind of fruit
As maids call medlars when they laugh alone.
O Romeo, that she were— O that she were
An open—etcetera; thou a poperin-pear!
Romeo, good night. I'll to my truckle-bed;
40 This field-bed is too cold for me to sleep.
Come, shall we go?
       Benvolio   Go then, for 'tis in vain
To seek him here that means not to be found.
                                          [*Exeunt*

Act 2   Scene 2

Romeo has climbed over the wall into
Capulet's orchard. He speaks aloud of
his love for Juliet, thinking that he is
alone. In fact Juliet has come out on to
the balcony of her bedroom, but at first
she is not aware of Romeo's presence
because her mind is so full of her own
thoughts. She too has fallen in love,
but she is very conscious of the fact
that Romeo is a Montague and belongs
to the family that is hated by her own
relatives. When Romeo speaks directly
to her, Juliet is at first embarrassed,
but she quickly loses her shyness and
exchanges promises of love and
marriage.

1   He (Mercutio) can laugh at the
injuries inflicted by love, because he
has never been hurt by love.

6   *her maid* : in classical mythology,
Diana, goddess of the Moon, was also
goddess of chastity; all virgins were her
maid-servants.

8   The uniform ('livery') worn by
Diana's virgins ('vestals') is a sickly
green. Young girls are often anaemic;
in Elizabethan times they were said to
be suffering from 'greensickness'.

Scene 2 *Verona : Capulet's orchard*

Enter Romeo

  Romeo
He jests at scars, that never felt a wound.
                    [Juliet *appears above at a window*
But, soft! What light through yonder window
   breaks?
It is the east, and Juliet is the sun!
Arise, fair sun, and kill the envious moon,
5 Who is already sick and pale with grief,
That thou her maid art far more fair than she.
Be not her maid, since she is envious;
Her vestal livery is but sick and green,
And none but fools do wear it; cast it off.
10 It is my lady. O, it is my love!
O that she knew she were!
She speaks, yet she says nothing: what of that?
Her eye discourses; I will answer it.
I am too bold, 'tis not to me she speaks:
15 Two of the fairest stars in all the heaven,
Having some business, do entreat her eyes
To twinkle in their spheres till they return.
What if her eyes were there, they in her head?
The brightness of her cheek would shame those
   stars

9   *fools*: professional jesters, whose uniform dress was a mixture of green and yellow.
11   *O that she knew she were*: I wish she knew that she is the girl I love.
13   *discourses*: speaks eloquently.
21   *airy region*: sky.

31   *lazy-pacing*: slow moving.

33   *wherefore art thou Romeo*: why are you called 'Romeo' (a name which shows he is a member of the Montague family)?
34   *Deny thy father*: refuse to acknowledge your family.

39   Romeo is still the same man, whatever his name.

46   *owes*: owns.
47   *doff*: shed.

52   *bescreen'd*: hidden.
53   *counsel*: private thoughts.

20   As daylight doth a lamp. Her eyes in heaven
       Would through the airy region stream so bright
       That birds would sing and think it were not night.
       See how she leans her cheek upon her hand:
       O that I were a glove upon that hand,
25   That I might touch that cheek.

       Juliet   Ay me!

       Romeo   She speaks!
       O speak again, bright angel—for thou art
       As glorious to this night, being o'er my head,
       As is a winged messenger of heaven
       Unto the white-upturned wond'ring eyes
30   Of mortals, that fall back to gaze on him
       When he bestrides the lazy-pacing clouds,
       And sails upon the bosom of the air.

       Juliet
       O Romeo, Romeo! wherefore art thou Romeo?
       Deny thy father, and refuse thy name;
35   Or, if thou wilt not, be but sworn my love,
       And I'll no longer be a Capulet.

       Romeo
       Shall I hear more, or shall I speak at this?

       Juliet
       'Tis but thy name that is my enemy;
       Thou art thyself, though not a Montague.
40   What's Montague? It is nor hand nor foot
       Nor arm nor face nor any other part
       Belonging to a man. O, be some other name!
       What's in a name? That which we call a rose
       By any other name would smell as sweet;
45   So Romeo would, were he not Romeo call'd,
       Retain that dear perfection which he owes
       Without that title. Romeo, doff thy name;
       And for thy name, which is no part of thee,
       Take all myself.

       Romeo   I take thee at thy word.
50   Call me but love, and I'll be new baptis'd;
       Henceforth I never will be Romeo.

       Juliet
       What man art thou, that, thus bescreen'd in night,
       So stumblest on my counsel?

Romeo   By a name
I know not how to tell thee who I am:
55 My name, dear saint, is hateful to myself,
Because it is an enemy to thee.
Had I it written, I would tear the word.
    Juliet
My ears have yet not drunk a hundred words
Of that tongue's utterance, yet I know the sound.
60 Art thou not Romeo, and a Montague?
    Romeo
Neither, fair maid, if either thee dislike.
    Juliet
How cam'st thou hither, tell me, and wherefore?
The orchard walls are high and hard to climb,
And the place death, considering who thou art,
65 If any of my kinsmen find thee here.
    Romeo
With love's light wings did I o'erperch these walls;
For stony limits cannot hold love out,
And what love can do, that dares love attempt;
Therefore thy kinsmen are no stop to me.
    Juliet
70 If they do see thee they will murder thee.
    Romeo
Alack, there lies more peril in thine eye
Than twenty of their swords! Look thou but sweet,
And I am proof against their enmity.
    Juliet
I would not for the world they saw thee here.
    Romeo
75 I have night's cloak to hide me from their eyes;
And but thou love me, let them find me here.
My life were better ended by their hate,
Than death prorogued, wanting of thy love.
    Juliet
By whose direction found'st thou out this place?
    Romeo
80 By love, that first did prompt me to inquire.
He lent me counsel, and I lent him eyes.
I am no pilot; yet, wert thou as far
As that vast shore wash'd with the farthest sea,
I would adventure for such merchandise.

61   *thee dislike* : displeases you.

66   *o'erperch* : fly over.
67   *limits* : boundaries.

69   *stop* : hindrance.

72   *Look thou but sweet* : if only you
will look on me with kindness.
73   *proof* : armed.

76   *but* : if only.

78   *prorogued* : postponed.
    wanting of : without.

81   *lent him eyes* : because love is
blind; see illustration, p. 10
82–4   I am not a sailor, but if you were
on the farthest coast, I would put to sea
('adventure') to gain such reward.

Juliet

85 Thou know'st the mask of night is on my face,
Else would a maiden blush bepaint my cheek
For that which thou has heard me speak tonight,
Fain would I dwell on form—fain, fain deny
What I have spoke. But farewell compliment!

90 Dost thou love me? I know thou wilt say 'Ay';
And I will take thy word. Yet, if thou swear'st,
Thou mayst prove false; at lovers' perjuries,
They say, Jove laughs. O gentle Romeo,
If thou dost love, pronounce it faithfully.

95 Or if thou think'st I am too quickly won,
I'll frown and be perverse and say thee nay,
So thou wilt woo; but else, not for the world.
In truth, fair Montague, I am too fond,
And therefore thou mayst think my 'haviour light.

100 But trust me, gentleman, I'll prove more true
Than those that have more cunning to be strange.
I should have been more strange, I must confess,
But that thou overheard'st, ere I was 'ware,
My true-love passion. Therefore pardon me,

105 And not impute this yielding to light love,
Which the dark night hath so discovered.

Romeo

Lady, by yonder blessed moon I vow
That tips with silver all these fruit-tree tops—

Juliet

O swear not by the moon, th' inconstant moon,

110 That monthly changes in her circled orb,
Lest that thy love prove likewise variable.

Romeo

What shall I swear by?

Juliet   Do not swear at all;
Or, if thou wilt, swear by thy gracious self,
Which is the god of my idolatry,

115 And I'll believe thee.

Romeo   If my heart's dear love—

Juliet

Well, do not swear. Although I joy in thee,
I have no joy of this contract to-night:
It is too rash, too unadvis'd, too sudden;
Too like the lightning, which doth cease to be

120 Ere one can say 'It lightens'. Sweet, good-night!

---

86   *maiden blush :* the blush of a
maiden.

88   *Fain would I :* I would like to.
          dwell on form : obey the rules.

89   *farewell compliment :* this is no
time for pretty phrases.

93   *Jove :* Jupiter, the chief of the
classical gods; he did not take lovers'
vows seriously, and merely laughed
when they were broken.

96   *say thee nay :* refuse you.

97   *So thou wilt woo :* provided that
you continue to court me.
          but else : but otherwise.

98   *fond :* foolish and affectionate.

99   *'haviour :* behaviour.
          light : immodest.

101   *have more cunning to be strange :*
are more clever and pretend to be
unmoved.

102   *should :* would.
          strange : reserved.

103   *But that :* if it were not for the
fact that.
          ware : aware.

104   *My true-love passion :* my
expression of true love.

105   Do not judge ('impute') this
surrender of mine to be a sign of
immodest love.

106   *discovered :* revealed.

110   *circled orb :* circular sphere (the
passage of the moon as it circles the
earth).

116   *joy :* rejoice.

117   *contract :* engagement.

This bud of love, by summer's ripening breath,
May prove a beauteous flower when next we meet.
Good-night, good-night! As sweet repose and rest
Come to thy heart as that within my breast!

Romeo

125 O, wilt thou leave me so unsatisfied?

Juliet

What satisfaction canst thou have to-night?

Romeo

Th' exchange of thy love's faithful vow for mine.

Juliet

I gave thee mine before thou didst request it;
And yet I would it were to give again.

Romeo

130 Wouldst thou withdraw it? For what purpose, love?

Juliet

But to be frank, and give it thee again.
And yet I wish but for the thing I have:
My bounty is as boundless as the sea,
My love as deep; the more I give to thee,

135 The more I have, for both are infinite.
                              [Nurse *calls within*
I hear some noise within. Dear love, adieu!
Anon, good Nurse! Sweet Montague, be true.
Stay but a little, I will come again.   [*Exit* Juliet

Romeo

O blessed, blessed night! I am afeard,

140 Being in night, all this is but a dream,
Too flattering-sweet to be substantial.

Enter Juliet *above*

Juliet

Three words, dear Romeo, and good-night indeed.
If that thy bent of love be honourable,
Thy purpose marriage, send me word tomorrow,

145 By one that I'll procure to come to thee,
Where and what time thou wilt perform the rite;
And all my fortunes at thy foot I'll lay,
And follow thee my lord throughout the world.

Nurse

[*Within*] Madam!

129   *I would :* I wish.

131   *frank :* generous.

137   *Anon :* I'm coming.

139   *afeard :* afraid.

141   *flattering-sweet :* delightfully attractive.
       substantial : real.

143   *bent :* intention.

146   *rite :* ceremony.

148   *follow thee my lord :* follow you as my lord.

Juliet

150 I come, anon.— But if thou mean'st not well.
I do beseech thee—

Nurse

[*Within*] Madam!

Juliet   By and by; I come—

To cease thy suit, and leave me to my grief.
Tomorrow will I send.

Romeo   So thrive my soul—

Juliet

A thousand times good-night!   [*Exit*

Romeo

155 A thousand times the worse, to want thy light!
Love goes towards love, as schoolboys from their
     books;
But love from love, toward school with heavy looks.

Enter Juliet *above*

Juliet

Hist! Romeo, hist! O for a falconer's voice,
To lure this tassel-gentle back again!

160 Bondage is hoarse, and may not speak aloud,
Else would I tear the cave where Echo lies,
And make her airy tongue more hoarse than mine,
With repetition of my Romeo's name.

Romeo

It is my soul that calls upon my name.

165 How silver-sweet sound lovers' tongues by night,
Like softest music to attending ears!

Juliet

Romeo!

Romeo   My nyas!

Juliet   What o'clock to-morrow

Shall I send to thee?

Romeo   By the hour of nine.

Juliet

I will not fail; 'tis twenty years till then.

170 I have forgot why I did call thee back.

Romeo

Let me stand here till thou remember it.

Juliet

I shall forget, to have thee still stand there,
Remembering how I love thy company.

151   *By and by* : presently.
152   *cease thy suit* : stop courting me.
153   *So thrive my soul* : as I hope my
      soul may thrive.
158   *a falconer's voice* : Juliet must
      whisper, but she longs to be able to call
      Romeo as a huntsman shouts to his
      hawks.

159   *tassel-gentle* : peregrine (the
      noblest of the falcons)
160   *Bondage* : Juliet is bound by the
      dangers of the situation; she cannot
      raise her voice, and therefore sounds
      'hoarse'.
161   *Else* : otherwise.
      Echo : a Greek nymph who pined
      away with love until all that was left of
      her was a voice in a cave.
162   *airy* : disembodied.
167   *nyas* : a young hawk that has not
      yet left the nest.
172   *still* : always.

Romeo
And I'll still stay, to have thee still forget,
175 Forgetting any other home but this.

Juliet
'Tis almost morning. I would have thee gone;
And yet no farther than a wanton's bird,
That lets it hop a little from her hand,
Like a poor prisoner in his twisted gyves,
180 And with a silken thread plucks it back again,
So loving-jealous of his liberty.

Romeo
I would I were thy bird.

Juliet   Sweet, so would I:
Yet I should kill thee with much cherishing.
Good-night, good-night! Parting is such sweet
     sorrow
185 That I shall say good-night till it be morrow.
                                              [*Exit*

Romeo
Sleep dwell upon thine eyes, peace in thy breast!
Would I were sleep and peace, so sweet to rest.
The grey-ey'd morn smiles on the frowning night,
Chequering the eastern clouds with streaks of
     light;
190 And darkness fleckled like a drunkard reels
From forth day's pathway, made by Titan's
     wheels.
Hence will I to my ghostly sire's close cell,
His help to crave and my dear hap to tell.   [*Exit*

177   *wanton :* playful (woman or
  child).
179   *gyves :* shackles.
180   *silken thread :* this was fastened
  round the bird's legs.
190   *fleckled :* dappled, with red
  patches (like a drunkard's face).
191   *From forth :* out of the way of.
        Titan's wheels : Hyperion, the
  Greek god of the sun, was
  sometimes called 'Titan'; he crossed
  the sky each day in his chariot, the sun.
192   *ghostly sire :* spiritual father.
193   *hap :* fortune.

Act 2   Scene 3
Gathering flowers outside his cell, the
hermit Friar Laurence meditates on
good and evil—in flowers and men. His
meditation is interrupted by Romeo,
who is excited about his love for Juliet.
Romeo insists that Friar Laurence
should perform a marriage ceremony:
and the Friar, although he is at first
reluctant, eventually sees that such a
marriage may be a means of uniting the
Montague and Capulet families.

1   *ere :* before.
        advance : sends out.

Scene 3 *Verona : Friar Laurence's cell*

Enter Friar Laurence *with a basket*

Friar Laurence
Now, ere the sun advance his burning eye
The day to cheer and night's dank dew to dry,
I must up-fill this osier cage of ours
With baleful weeds and precious-juiced flowers.
5 The earth that's nature's mother is her tomb;
What is her burying grave, that is her womb;
And from her womb children of divers kind
We sucking on her natural bosom find.

3   *osier cage :* willow basket.
4   *baleful :* harmful.
7   *divers :* different.
10 *None but for some :* all have some virtues.
11 *mickle :* much.
    grace : divine virtue.
15 *strain'd :* forced, perverted.
16 *stumbling on abuse :* finding some harmful application.
17–18   Good can become evil, when it is badly used; and evil can sometimes be made good, by the right action.
    sometime's : sometime is.
    dignified : made worthy.
19 *infant rind :* tender skin, bud.
20 There is a place of poison, and also the healing power of medicine.
21 With its scent, the flower cheers each part of the (human) body.
22 When the plant is eaten, it stops all the senses by stopping the heart.
23 *still :* always.
24 *grace :* i.e. divine grace.
26 *canker :* cancer.

27 *Benedicite :* God bless you.
29 *argues :* suggests.
    distemper'd : disturbed.
30 *bid good morrow to :* say goodbye, to, get up from.
31 *Care . . . watch :* care is like a watchman, who never sleeps.

Many for many virtues excellent,
10 None but for some, and yet all different.
    O mickle is the powerful grace that lies
    In plants, herbs, stones, and their true qualities.
    For naught so vile that on the earth doth live
    But to the earth some special good doth give;
15 Nor aught so good but, strain'd from that fair use,
    Revolts from true birth, stumbling on abuse.
    Virtue itself turns vice, being misapplied,
    And vice sometime's by action dignified.
    Within the infant rind of this weak flower
20 Poison hath residence, and medicine power:
    For this, being smelt, with that part cheers each part;
    Being tasted, stays all senses with the heart.
    Two such opposed kings encamp them still
    In man as well as herbs—grace and rude will.
25 And where the worser is predominant,
    Full soon the canker death eats up that plant.

Enter Romeo

Romeo
Good morrow, father!
Friar Laurence   *Benedicite!*
What early tongue so sweet saluteth me?
Young son, it argues a distemper'd head
30 So soon to bid good morrow to thy bed.
    Care keeps his watch in every old man's eye,

33   *unbruised* : unharmed (by experience).
       unstuff'd : untroubled.
34   *couch* : rest.
36   *distemperature* : disorder, uneasiness.
37   *hit* : guess.

And where care lodges, sleep will never lie.
But where unbruised youth with unstuff'd brain
Doth couch his limbs, there golden sleep doth reign.
35 Therefore thy earliness doth me assure
   Thou art up-rous'd with some distemperature;
   Or if not so, then here I hit it right:
   Our Romeo hath not been in bed tonight.
       Romeo
   That last is true; the sweeter rest was mine.
       Friar Laurence
40 God pardon sin! Wast thou with Rosaline?
       Romeo

41   *ghostly* : spiritual.
42   *that name's woe* : the misery that I suffered because of the name 'Rosaline'.

   With Rosaline, my ghostly father? No;
   I have forgot that name, and that name's woe.
       Friar Laurence
   That's my good son! But where hast thou been then?
       Romeo
   I'll tell thee, ere thou ask it me again.
45 I have been feasting with mine enemy,
   Where on a sudden one hath wounded me,
   That's by me wounded. Both our remedies

47   *Both our remedies* : cures for both of us.

   Within thy help and holy physic lies.
   I bear no hatred, blessed man; for, lo,
50 My intercession likewise steads my foe.
       Friar Laurence

50   *intercession* : prayer, petition.
       steads : benefits.
51   *homely* : simple.
       thy drift : what you say.
52   *Riddling* : ambiguous, difficult to understand.
       shrift : absolution.
53   *plainly* : simply.

   Be plain, good son, and homely in thy drift;
   Riddling confession finds but riddling shrift.
       Romeo
   Then plainly know my heart's dear love is set
   On the fair daughter of rich Capulet:
55 As mine on hers, so hers is set on mine;
   And all combin'd, save what thou must combine
   By holy marriage. When, and where, and how
   We met, we woo'd, and made exchange of vow,
   I'll tell thee as we pass; but this I pray,

59   *pass* : go along.

60 That thou consent to marry us today.
       Friar Laurence
   Holy Saint Francis, what a change is here!
   Is Rosaline, whom thou didst love so dear,
   So soon forsaken? Young men's love then lies
   Not truly in their hearts, but in their eyes.

65 *Jesu Maria :* by Jesus and Mary.
a deal of brine : a lot of salt water.

68 *to season love :* to give a flavour
(by adding salt) to love.
that of it doth not taste : that now
has no flavour.

73 When you were your former self,
with your old miseries.

75 *sentence :* maxim, wise saying.

76 Women can be excused for being
weak, since men are no stronger.

77 *chid'st :* scolded.

82 *allow :* return.

84 *by rote :* from memory.

89 *stand :* insist.

65 Jesu Maria! What a deal of brine
Hath wash'd thy sallow cheeks for Rosaline;
How much salt water thrown away in waste,
To season love, that of it doth not taste!
The sun not yet thy sighs from heaven clears,
70 Thy old groans yet ring in my ancient ears.
Lo, here upon thy cheek the stain doth sit
Of an old tear that is not wash'd off yet.
If e'er thou wast thyself and these woes thine,
Thou and these woes were all for Rosaline.
75 And art thou chang'd? Pronounce this sentence
  then :
Women may fall, when there's no strength in men.
    Romeo
Thou chid'st me oft for loving Rosaline.
    Friar Laurence
For doting, not for loving, pupil mine.
    Romeo
And bad'st me bury love.
    Friar Laurence   Not in a grave,
80 To lay one in, another out to have.
    Romeo
I pray thee, chide me not. Her I love now
Doth grace for grace and love for love allow.
The other did not so.
    Friar Laurence   O, she knew well
Thy love did read by rote, that could not spell.
85 But come, young waverer, come, go with me,
In one respect I'll thy assistant be.
For this alliance may so happy prove,
To turn your households' rancour to pure love.
    Romeo
O let us hence! I stand on sudden haste.
    Friar Laurence
90 Wisely and slow : they stumble that run fast.
                                        [*Exeunt*

Act 2   Scene 4

Tybalt, Juliet's cousin, has challenged
Romeo to fight a duel with him;
Benvolio and Mercutio discuss Tybalt,
and find further amusement in
Romeo's love for Rosaline. Romeo
comes along and shares in their fun.
Whilst all three are laughing together
the Nurse comes in search of Romeo.
She has been sent by Juliet to find out
what his intentions are.

11   *answer the letter's master* : i.e.
respond to the challenge by consenting
to fight.

11–12   *how . . . dared* : having been
challenged ('dared') to fight, he will
show Tybalt how courageous he is
(how he 'dares' to fight).

14   *run through* : pierced.

15   *pin* : the peg marking the centre
of the target used for archery practice.

16   *blind bow-boy* : Cupid.
      butt-shaft : arrow.

19   *Prince of Cats* : Mercutio alludes
to a character in various animal stories
of the sixteenth century, who was
indeed a prince among cats.

20   *captain of compliments* : master of
formalities.

21   *prick-song* : printed music (sung
with more accuracy than tunes sung
from memory).
      time : rhythm.

22   *distance* : the correct distance
between two swordsmen (or between
two notes in music).

22   *proportion* : balance.
      minim : the shortest note in
music; Mercutio means that Tybalt
(when he is fighting) makes two
movements with his sword, pausing for
a very brief moment after each thrust,
and then pierces to the heart with his
third stroke.

23–4   *The very . . . button* : Tybalt
fences with such accuracy that he is
easily able to slice his opponent's
buttons in two.

25   *house* : rank (or school of
fencing).

Scene 4   *Verona*

Enter Benvolio *and* Mercutio

Mercutio
Where the devil should this Romeo be? Came he
not home to night?

Benvolio
Not to his father's; I spoke with his man.

Mercutio
Why, that same pale hard-hearted wench, that
5 Rosaline, torments him so, that he will sure run mad.

Benvolio
Tybalt, the kinsman of old Capulet, hath sent a
letter to his father's house.

Mercutio
A challenge, on my life.

Benvolio
Romeo will answer it.

Mercutio
10 Any man that can write may answer a letter.

Benvolio
Nay, he will answer the letter's master, how he
dares, being dared.

Mercutio
Alas, poor Romeo, he is already dead! Stabbed
with a white wench's black eye; run through the ear
15 with a love-song; the very pin of his heart cleft with
the blind bow-boy's butt-shaft. And is he a man to
encounter Tybalt?

Benvolio
Why, what is Tybalt?

Mercutio
More than Prince of Cats, I can tell you. O, he is
20 the courageous captain of compliments. He fights as
you sing prick-song: keeps time, distance, and
proportion. He rests his minim rests, one, two, and
the third in your bosom. The very butcher of a
silk button. A duellist, a duellist! A gentleman of
25 the very first house, of the first and second cause.
Ah, the immortal *passado*! the *punto reverso*! the
hay!

25   *first and second cause :* the different schools of fencing taught their pupils that they must only fight when they had proper causes. Two principal causes were (a) being accused of a major crime; and (b) matters of personal or family honour. The second of these gives Tybalt his reason for challenging Romeo.

26–7   *passado . . . hay :* technical terms for various fencing movements. The *passado* is a forward thrust; *punto reverso* a back-handed blow; and the *hay* (from Italian '*hai*' = 'you have it') is the stab to the heart.

28   *The pox of :* a plague on.
  antic : absurd.
  affecting fantasticoes : would-be eccentrics.

29   *new tuners of accents :* affected speakers.
  '*By Jesu . . .' :* Mercutio imitates the speakers.

30   *blade :* sword.
  tall : fine.

31   *grandsire :* grandfather; Mercutio addresses Benvolio, speaking as one old-fashioned man to another.

32   *strange :* foreign

33   *fashion-mongers :* followers of fashion (in dress and language).
  pardon-mes : a phrase used excessively (Mercutio thinks) by those who pretend to be fashionable.

34   *stand so much on :* think so much about.
  form : manner; Mercutio proceeds with a pun on 'form' = seat.

35   *at ease :* in comfort.
  O, their bones . . . : they cry out that their bones ache because they are not so comfortable sitting on the 'new form' as they were on the 'old bench'.

38   *roe :* (a) the first syllable of his name (reducing it to 'me—O'; the cry of a despairing lover is 'O me'); (b) deer (a pun on 'dear'); (c) reproductive organs of a male fish.
  dried herring : Mercutio develops sense (c) of *roe*; the roe is removed from a herring when it is dried.

Benvolio
The what?
  Mercutio
The pox of such antic, lisping, affecting fantasticoes, these new tuners of accents! 'By Jesu, a very
30 good blade! a very tall man! a very good whore'.
Why, is not this a lamentable thing, grandsire, that
we should be thus afflicted with these strange flies,
these fashion-mongers, these 'pardon-mes', who
stand so much on the new form that they cannot sit
35 at ease on the old bench? O, their bones, their
bones!

Enter Romeo

  Benvolio
Here comes Romeo, here comes Romeo!
  Mercutio
Without his roe, like a dried herring. O flesh, flesh,

39   *fishified*: turned into fish (a limp, dried herring).

        numbers: verses, poetry.

40   *Petrarch*: an Italian poet of the fourteenth century.

        flowed: wrote.

        Laura: the lady whom Petrarch loved.

        to his lady: compared with Romeo's mistress.

41   *love*: lover.

        be-rhyme: write poetry (rhymes) about her.

42-3   Mercutio names some of the famous women of myth and history. The stories of Dido (queen of Carthage) and Hero (priestess of Sestos) were told by Shakespeare's great contemporary, Christopher Marlowe; both Marlowe and Shakespeare portrayed Helen of Troy (in *Dr Faustus* and in *Troilus and Cressida* respectively); Shakespeare wrote the serious tragedy *Antony and Cleopatra*, describing the love of the queen of Egypt for the Roman soldier. The comic tragedy 'Pyramus and Thisbe' is a parody of heroic tragedy in Shakespeare's play *A Midsummer Night's Dream*, which was written at much the same time as *Romeo and Juliet*.

42   *dowdy*: plain, nondescript woman.

        gipsy: brown creature.

43   *hildings*: prostitutes.

44   *not to the purpose*: nothing important.

        bon jour: good day.

46   *slop*: wide trousers (especially fashionable in France); presumably Romeo is still wearing his costume for the masque.

        gave us the counterfeit: cheated us.

49   *slip*: a slang term for counterfeit coin.

        conceive: understand.

50   *great*: important.

51   *case*: situation.

        strain: forgo.

---

how art thou fishified! Now is he for the numbers
40 that Petrarch flowed in: Laura, to his lady, was a
kitchen-wench—marry, she had a better love to be-
rhyme her! Dido a dowdy, Cleopatra a gipsy, Helen
and Hero hildings and harlots; Thisbe, a grey eye
or so, but not to the purpose. Signor Romeo, *bon*
45 *jour*! There's a French salutation to your French
slop. You gave us the counterfeit fairly last night.

Romeo

Good morrow to you both. What counterfeit did I
give you?

Mercutio

The slip, sir, the slip. Can you not conceive?

Romeo

50 Pardon, good Mercutio, my business was great;
and in such a case as mine a man may strain
courtesy.

Mercutio

That's as much as to say, such a case as yours
constrains a man to bow in the hams.

Romeo

55 Meaning—to curtsy.

54 *bow in the hams :* bend in the knees.

56 *kindly :* properly.
hit it : got the meaning.

58 *pink :* (a) perfect example; (b) a flower; (c) pattern made with holes in leather.

59 Romeo selects one meaning of the word 'pink'.

61 If 'pink' is a flower, then his shoe ('pump') is well decorated with flowers.

66 A very thin ('single-soled') joke, which is odd ('singular') only ('solely') because there is no other (for its 'singleness').

68 *Come between us :* Mercutio calls to Benvolio (as though he were a supporter in a fencing-match) to come to his aid in the verbal contest.

69 *Switch and spurs :* use the whip and spurs on your wit (as though it were a horse in a race).

69 70 *cry a match :* declare that I have won.

71 *wild-goose chase :* a horse-race in which the leader chooses a course and the other riders must follow him wherever he goes.

72 *goose :* fool.

73 *whole five :* i.e. five wits; these are (traditionally) common-sense, memory, imagination, fancy, and judgement.

74 *was I with you there :* did I score a point then?

76 *for the goose :* as a fool.

77 *bite thee by the ear :* a sign of affection.

79 *sweeting :* sweet apple, used for making sauce (apple sauce is traditionally served with roast goose).

81 *well served in to :* properly served with.

Mercutio
Thou hast most kindly hit it.

Romeo
A most courteous exposition.

Mercutio
Nay, I am the very pink of courtesy.

Romeo
Pink for flower.

Mercutio
60 Right.

Romeo
Why, then is my pump well flowered.

Mercutio
Sure wit! Follow me this jest now till thou hast worn out the pump, that, when the single sole of it is worn, the jest may remain after the wearing,
65 solely singular.

Romeo
O single-soled jest, solely singular for the singleness!

Mercutio
Come between us, good Benvolio; my wits faints.

Romeo
Switch and spurs, switch and spurs—or I'll cry a
70 match.

Mercutio
Nay, if our wits run the wild-goose chase, I have done; for thou hast more of the wild goose in one of thy wits than, I am sure, I have in my whole five. Was I with you there for the goose?

Romeo
75 Thou wast never with me for anything when thou wast not there for the goose.

Mercutio
I will bite thee by the ear for that jest.

Romeo
Nay, good goose, bite not.

Mercutio
Thy wit is a very bitter sweeting; it is a most sharp
80 sauce.

Romeo
And is it not, then, well served in to a sweet goose?

82   *cheverel* : the soft skin of a young goat which stretches easily—as the word starts with the 'ch' of 'inch' and ends with 'l'. Mercutio is in effect saying 'you can make your little wit go a long way'.

83   *ell* : 45 inches.

84   *I stretch it out* : I'll make it go even further.
      broad : (a) wide; (b) obvious; (c) indecent.

89   *by art* : by skill.

90   *natural* : idiot.

91   *lolling* : with his tongue hanging out.
      to hide : trying to hide.
      bauble : coxcomb—the decorated stick carried by a professional jester.

93   *against the hair* : against the grain, unnaturally.

94   *else* : otherwise.

98   *goodly gear* : fine business.

99   *A sail, a sail* : the cry of fisherman when a boat is perceived on the horizon; presumably Romeo alludes to the Nurse's appearance.

100   *smock* : dress
102   *Anon* : I'm coming.

106   *God ye good morrow* : may God give you a good morning.

Mercutio
O, here's a wit of cheverel, that stretches from an inch narrow to an ell broad!

Romeo
I stretch it out for that word 'broad', which added
85 to the goose, proves thee far and wide a broad goose.

Mercutio
Why, is this not better now than groaning for love? Now art thou sociable, now art thou Romeo; now art thou what thou art, by art as well as by nature:
90 for this drivelling love is like a great natural, that runs lolling up and down to hide his bauble in a hole.

Benvolio
Stop there, stop there!

Mercutio
Thou desirest me to stop in my tale against the hair.

Benvolio
Thou wouldst else have made thy tale large.

Mercutio
95 O, thou art deceived! I would have made it short; for I was come to the whole depth of my tale, and meant indeed to occupy the argument no longer.

Romeo
Here's goodly gear!

Enter Nurse *and* Peter

A sail, a sail!

Mercutio
100 Two, two; a shirt and a smock.

Nurse
Peter!

Peter
Anon!

Nurse
My fan, Peter.

Mercutio
Good Peter, to hide her face; for her fan's the fairer
105 face.

Nurse
God ye good morrow, gentlemen.

107   *God ye good e'en*: may God give
       you a good evening (i.e. afternoon).

110   *dial*: clock.
       prick: point.

111   *Out upon you*: the Nurse appears
       to be shocked.
       What . . . you: what sort of man
       are you?

113   *mar*: spoil.

114   *By my troth*: upon my word.

115   *quoth 'a*: says he.

119   *fault*: want.

122   *took*: understood.

124   *confidence*: the Nurse means
       'conference' (= talk).

125   *indite*: Benvolio makes the
       deliberate mistake of saying 'indite' (=
       write) for 'invite'.

126   *bawd*: (a) keeper of a brothel; (b)
       hare.
       So ho: the cry of a huntsman,
       when he has sighted the object of the
       chase.

128   *lenten pie*: Lent was the time of
       fasting (before Easter) when no meat
       could be eaten.

129   *hoar*: old (with a pun on
       'whore').
       spent: eaten.

134   *too much for a score*: not worth
       paying for.

Mercutio
God ye good e'en, fair gentlewoman.

Nurse
Is it good e'en?

Mercutio
'Tis no less, I tell you; for the bawdy hand of the
110 dial is now upon the prick of noon.

Nurse
Out upon you! What a man are you!

Romeo
One, gentlewoman, that God hath made, for
himself to mar.

Nurse
By my troth, it is well said; 'for himself to mar',
115 quoth 'a?—Gentlemen, can any of you tell me
where I may find the young Romeo?

Romeo
I can tell you; but young Romeo will be older when
you have found him than he was when you sought
him. I am the youngest of that name, for fault of a
120 worse.

Nurse
You say well.

Mercutio
Yea, is the worst well? Very well took, i' faith;
wisely, wisely.

Nurse
If you be he, sir, I desire some confidence with you.

Benvolio
125 She will indite him to some supper.

Mercutio
A bawd, a bawd, a bawd! So ho!

Romeo
What hast thou found?

Mercutio
No hare, sir; unless a hare, sir, in a lenten pie, that
is something stale and hoar ere it be spent.
                                    [*He walks round them and sings*

130   An old hare hoar
           And an old hare hoar
         Is very good meat in Lent.
           But a hare that is hoar
           Is too much for a score

135   When it hoars ere it be spent.
Romeo, will you come to your father's? We'll to
dinner thither.
        Romeo
I will follow you.
        Mercutio
Farewell, ancient lady; farewell,
140   'Lady, lady, lady'.
                    [*Exeunt* Mercutio *and* Benvolio
        Nurse
I pray you, sir, what saucy merchant was this, that
was so full of his ropery?
        Romeo
A gentleman, Nurse, that loves to hear himself talk,
and will speak more in a minute than he will stand
145   to in a month.
        Nurse
And 'a speak anything against me, I'll take him
down, and 'a were lustier than he is, and twenty such
jacks; and if I cannot, I'll find those that shall.
Scurvy knave! I am none of his flirt-gills; I am
150   none of his skains-mates. [*To* Peter] And thou must
stand by too, and suffer every knave to use me at his
pleasure!
        Peter
I saw no man use you at his pleasure; if I had, my
weapon should quickly have been out, I warrant
155   you. I dare draw as soon as another man, if I see
occasion in a good quarrel, and the law on my side.
        Nurse
Now, afore God, I am so vexed, that every part
about me quivers. Scurvy knave! Pray you, sir, a
word—and as I told you, my young lady bid me
160   inquire you out. What she bid me say I will keep to
myself. But first let me tell ye, if ye should lead her
in a fool's paradise, as they say, it were a very gross
kind of behaviour, as they say; for the gentlewoman
is young; and, therefore, if you should deal double
165   with her, truly it were an ill thing to be offered to
any gentlewoman, and very weak dealing.
        Romeo
Nurse, commend me to thy lady and mistress. I
protest unto thee—

140   Mercutio sings the chorus of a popular song.

142   *ropery :* roguery (= jokes).

144   *speak :* promise.
        stand to : perform.

146   *And 'a :* if he.
        take him down : lower his pride.
148   *jacks :* fellows.
149   *Scurvy knave :* rotten chap.
        flirt-gills : loose women.
150   *skains-mates :* fighting companions ('skains' were long Irish knives).
151   *suffer :* allow.
        use me at his pleasure : do as he likes with me.

161–2   *lead ... paradise :* take advantage of her.

164   *deal double :* deceive.

167   *commend me :* give my greetings.
168   *protest unto thee :* promise you.

Nurse

Good heart, and, i' faith, I will tell her as much.
170 Lord, Lord! She will be a joyful woman.

Romeo

What wilt thou tell her, Nurse? Thou dost not
mark me.

172   *mark :* listen to.

Nurse

I will tell her, sir, that you do protest; which, as I
take it, is a gentlemanlike offer.

Romeo

175 Bid her devise
Some means to come to shrift this afternoon;
And there she shall at Friar Laurence' cell,
Be shriv'd and married. Here is for thy pains.
                              [*Offers money*

176   *shrift :* confession.

178   *shriv'd :* be given absolution
(confession–with absolution–is
necessary before the sacrament of
marriage can be received).
        pains : trouble.

Nurse

No, truly, sir; not a penny.

Romeo

180 Go to; I say, you shall.

Nurse

This afternoon, sir? Well, she shall be there.

Romeo

And stay, good Nurse, behind the abbey wall.
Within this hour my man shall be with thee,
And bring thee cords made like a tackled stair,
185 Which to the high top-gallant of my joy
Must be my convoy in the secret night.
Farewell! Be trusty, and I'll quit thy pains.
Farewell! Commend me to thy mistress.

184   *cords :* rope.
       tackled stair : ship's ladder (i.e. a
rope ladder).
185   *top-gallant :* the platform at the
top of a ship's mast.
186   *convoy :* means of access.
187   *quit :* requite, reward.

Nurse

Now God in heaven bless thee! Hark you, sir.

Romeo

190 What sayest thou, my dear Nurse?

Nurse

Is your man secret? Did you ne'er hear say
Two may keep counsel, putting one away?

191   *secret :* to be trusted.
192   Two people can keep a secret,
but not three.
195   *prating :* chattering.
196   *would fain :* would very much like
to.
197   *lay knife aboard :* claim Juliet for
his bride. Elizabethan guests brought
their own knives to dinner and set
them on the table to mark their places
and make sure that they were served
with food.

Romeo

I warrant thee my man's as true as steel.

Nurse

Well, sir; my mistress is the sweetest lady—Lord,
195 Lord!—when 'twas a little prating thing—O, there
is a nobleman in town, one Paris, that would fain
lay knife aboard; but she, good soul, had as lief see a

198   *I anger her sometimes :* the Nurse has not really been given time in the play to tease Juliet in this way!
199   *the properer :* the more handsome.
200–1   *pale as any clout :* white as any sheet.
201   *the versal world :* the whole (universal) world.
         rosemary : the herb of remembrance, worn at weddings and funerals.
202   *with a letter :* with the same letter; like Capulet's Servant in *Act 1, Scene 2,* the Nurse cannot read.
204   *'the dog's name' :* the letter 'R' was called the dog-letter because it makes the sound of a dog growling.
206   *sententious :* the Nurse means 'sentence' (= proverb or witty saying).

211   *Before, and apace :* go in front of me, and walk fast.

toad, a very toad, as see him. I anger her sometimes and tell her that Paris is the properer man; but, I'll
200   warrant you, when I say so, she looks as pale as any clout in the versal world. Doth not rosemary and Romeo begin both with a letter?

Romeo

Ay, nurse: what of that? Both with an 'R'.

Nurse

Ah, mocker! That's the dog's name. 'R' is for the—
205   No; I know it begins with some other letter: and she had the prettiest sententious of it, of you and rosemary, that it would do you good to hear it.

Romeo

Commend me to thy lady.   [*Exit*

Nurse

Ay, a thousand times. Peter!

Peter

210   Anon!

Nurse

Before, and apace.   [*Exeunt*

Act 2   Scene 5

Juliet anxiously waits for the Nurse, who arrives breathless and complaining of the tiring journey she has had. After teasing Juliet, the Nurse tells her of Romeo's plans for their marriage.

3   *Perchance :* perhaps.

6   *louring :* gloomy.
7   *nimble-pinion'd doves :* swift-winged doves, which in classical mythology draw the chariot of Venus, goddess of love.
8   *wind-swift :* swift as the wind.
9   *highmost hill :* at the height.
12   *affections :* desires.
       blood : passion.
13–15   Juliet wishes that the Nurse could be like a tennis ball, so that she and Romeo—like two tennis players— could strike ('bandy') her between them.

Scene 5 *Verona : Capulet's house*

Enter Juliet

Juliet

The clock struck nine when I did send the Nurse;
In half an hour she promis'd to return.
Perchance she cannot meet him! That's not so.
O, she is lame! Love's heralds should be thoughts,
5   Which ten times faster glide than the sun's beams
Driving back shadows over louring hills:
Therefore do nimble-pinion'd doves draw Love,
And therefore hath the wind-swift Cupid wings.
Now is the sun upon the highmost hill
10   Of this day's journey, and from nine till twelve
Is three long hours, yet she is not come.
Had she affections, and warm youthful blood,
She would be as swift in motion as a ball:
My words would bandy her to my sweet love,
15   And his to me.
But old folks, many feign as they were dead:
Unwieldy, slow, heavy and pale as lead.

Enter Nurse *and* Peter

O God, she comes! O honey Nurse, what news?
Hast thou met with him? Send thy man away.

Nurse

20 Peter, stay at the gate.   [*Exit* Peter

Juliet

Now, good sweet Nurse— O Lord, why look'st
   thou sad?
Though news be sad, yet tell them merrily.
If good, thou sham'st the music of sweet news
By playing it to me with so sour a face.

Nurse

25 I am aweary, give me leave awhile:
Fie, how my bones ache! What a jaunt have I had!

Juliet

I would thou hadst my bones and I thy news.
Nay come, I pray thee, speak; good, good Nurse,
   speak.

Nurse

Jesu, what haste! Can you not stay awhile?
30 Do you not see that I am out of breath?

Juliet

How art thou out of breath when thou hast breath
To say to me that thou art out of breath?
The excuse that thou dost make in this delay
Is longer than the tale thou dost excuse.
35 Is thy news good, or bad? Answer to that.
Say either, and I'll stay the circumstance:
Let me be satisfied, is 't good or bad?

Nurse

Well, you have made a simple choice; you know not
   how to choose a man. Romeo? No, not he. Though
40 his face be better than any man's, yet his leg excels
all men's; and for a hand, and a foot, and a body,
though they be not to be talked on, yet they are past
compare. He is not the flower of courtesy, but, I'll
warrant him, as gentle as a lamb. Go thy ways,
45 wench! Serve God. What, have you dined at home?

Juliet

No, no. But all this did I know before.
What says he of our marriage? What of that?

---

22   *news :* this noun could be either singular or plural in the sixteenth century.

26   *jaunt :* exhausting trip.

29   *stay :* wait.

33   *in this delay :* for this delay.

36   *stay the circumstance :* wait for the details.

38   *simple :* foolish.

42   *not to be talked on :* not worth talking about.

43   *flower :* model.

44   *Go thy ways :* away you go.

Nurse

Lord, how my head aches! What a head have I!
It beats as it would fall in twenty pieces.

50 My back o' t'other side—O, my back, my back!
Beshrew your heart for sending me about,
To catch my death with jaunting up and down.

Juliet

I' faith, I am sorry that thou art not well.
Sweet, sweet, sweet Nurse, tell me, what says my
    love?

Nurse

55 Your love says, like an honest gentleman, and a
courteous, and a kind, and a handsome, and, I
warrant, a virtuous—Where is your mother?

Juliet

Where is my mother? Why, she is within;
Where should she be? How oddly thou repliest:

60 'Your love says, like an honest gentleman,
"Where is your mother?"'

Nurse   O God's lady dear,

Are you so hot? Marry, come up, I trow;
Is this the poultice for my aching bones?
Henceforward do your messages yourself.

Juliet

65 Here's such a coil! Come, what says Romeo?

Nurse

Have you got leave to go to shrift today?

Juliet

I have.

Nurse

Then hie you hence to Friar Laurence' cell,
There stays a husband to make you a wife.

70 Now comes the wanton blood up in your cheeks,
They'll be in scarlet straight at any news.
Hie you to church. I must another way,
To fetch a ladder, by the which your love
Must climb a bird's nest soon when it is dark.

75 I am the drudge, and toil in your delight,
But you shall bear the burden soon at night.
Go—I'll to dinner: hie you to the cell.

Juliet

Hie to high fortune! Honest Nurse, farewell.

[*Exeunt*

---

50 *o' t'other side :* on the other side.
51 *Beshrew :* curse.
52 *jaunting :* tripping.

55 *honest :* honourable.

61 *God's lady :* i.e. the Virgin Mary.
62 *hot :* impatient.

65 *coil :* fuss.
66 *shrift :* confession.

68 *hie :* go.

70 *wanton :* uncontrolled.
71 *be in scarlet :* i.e. blush.

75 *toil in your delight :* labour for
your happiness.

Act 2   Scene 6

The lovers meet at Friar Laurence's cell.

1–2   May heaven look favourably upon this act, so that the future ('after-hours') does not reproach ('chide') us by bringing sorrow.

4   *countervail* : equal.

6   *Do thou but close our hands* : all you have to do is join our hands.

8   *but* : only.

10   *powder* : gun-powder.

12   *his* : its.
13   Eating it destroys the desire for the honey.

15   *tardy* : late.

18   *bestride* : ride upon
    gossamers : spiders' webs.
19   *idles* : floats.
    wanton : playful.
20   *light* : trivial
    vanity : the pleasures of this world; see Ecclesiastes, 1:2 and 2:1.
21   *ghostly* : spiritual.

23   Juliet must give the greeting to Romeo as well as the Friar, otherwise he will be giving her excessive thanks; perhaps she kisses him.
26   *blazon* : describe (the metaphor is taken from heraldry).
27   *neighbour* : surrounding.
28   *Unfold* : express.
29   *in either* : from each other.

Scene 6 *Verona : Friar Laurence's cell*

Enter Friar Laurence *and* Romeo

Friar Laurence
So smile the heaven, upon this holy act,
That after-hours with sorrow chide us not!
    Romeo
Amen, amen! But come what sorrow can,
It cannot countervail the exchange of joy
5 That one short minute gives me in her sight.
Do thou but close our hands with holy words,
Then love-devouring death do what he dare;
It is enough I may but call her mine.
    Friar Laurence
These violent delights have violent ends,
10 And in their triumph die, like fire and powder
Which as they kiss consume. The sweetest honey
Is loathsome in his own deliciousness,
And in the taste confounds the appetite:
Therefore love moderately—long love doth so:
15 Too swift arrives as tardy as too slow.

Enter Juliet

Here comes the lady: O, so light a foot
Will ne'er wear out the everlasting flint:
A lover may bestride the gossamers
That idles in the wanton summer air,
20 And yet not fall: so light is vanity.
    Juliet
Good even to my ghostly confessor.
    Friar Laurence
Romeo shall thank thee, daughter, for us both.
    Juliet
As much to him, else is his thanks too much.
    Romeo
Ah Juliet, if the measure of thy joy
25 Be heap'd like mine, and that thy skill be more
To blazon it, then sweeten with thy breath
This neighbour air, and let rich music's tongue
Unfold the imagin'd happiness that both
Receive in either by this dear encounter.

30   *Conceit :* imagination.
      matter : substance, reality.
32   Those who can say how much
money they have are not really rich.

34   *sum up sum :* add up the total.

36   *by your leaves :* with your
permission.

Juliet

30 Conceit, more rich in matter than in words,
      Brags of his substance, not of ornament.
      They are but beggars that can count their worth;
      But my true love is grown to such excess
      I cannot sum up sum of half my wealth.
Friar Laurence
35 Come, come with me, and we will make short work;
      For, by your leaves, you shall not stay alone
      Till holy church incorporate two in one.   [*Exeunt*

Act 3

Act 3 Scene 1

Mercutio teases Benvolio, and tries to make fun of Tybalt. But Tybalt is determined to challenge Romeo to a duel. When Romeo refuses the challenge, Mercutio draws his sword; in the fighting that follows, both Mercutio and Tybalt are killed. Once again (as in *Act 1*, Scene 1) the citizens of Verona rush to the scene, and the Prince pronounces a sentence of banishment.

1	*retire :* go indoors.
2	*Capels :* Capulets.
	abroad : out of doors.
3	*'scape :* avoid.
	brawl : quarrel.
6	*claps me :* throws.
8	*by . . . cup :* by the time the second cup of wine has started to work on him (making him drunk).
9	*draws him :* draws his sword.
	on : against.
	drawer : waiter, barman.
11	*jack :* chap.
	mood : temper.
12	*moved to be moody :* provoked to be angry.
13	*moody to be moved :* angry at being provoked.
15	*and :* if.
20	*hazel eyes :* eyes the colour of a hazel nut.
23	*meat :* food.

Scene 1 *Verona*

Enter Mercutio, Benvolio, Page, *and* Servants

Benvolio

I pray thee, good Mercutio, let's retire:
The day is hot, the Capels are abroad,
And, if we meet, we shall not 'scape a brawl,
For now, these hot days, is the mad blood stirring.

Mercutio

5 Thou art like one of these fellows that, when he enters the confines of a tavern, claps me his sword upon the table and says, 'God send me no need of thee!', and by the operation of the second cup draws him on the drawer, when, indeed, there is no need.

Benvolio

10 Am I like such a fellow?

Mercutio

Come, come, thou art as hot a jack in thy mood as any in Italy; and as soon moved to be moody, and as soon moody to be moved.

Benvolio

And what to?

Mercutio

15 Nay, and there were two such, we should have none shortly, for one would kill the other. Thou! Why, thou wilt quarrel with a man that hath a hair more or a hair less in his beard than thou hast. Thou wilt quarrel with a man for cracking nuts, having no 20 other reason but because thou hast hazel eyes. What eye but such an eye would spy out such a quarrel? Thy head is as full of quarrels as an egg is full of meat; and yet thy head hath been beaten as

24   *addle* : rotten.

27   *fall out* : quarrel.
28   *doublet* : sleeveless jacket;
traditionally, Easter is the time for
wearing new clothes.
30   *riband* : ribbon, shoe-laces; new
shoes should have new laces.
     tutor me from quarrelling : teach
me to stop quarrelling.
31   *apt* : ready.
32   *fee simple* : absolute possession (a
legal term); Benvolio is saying that his
life would not last an hour and a
quarter if Mercutio's accusation were
correct.

44   *consort'st* : are associated.

45   *Consort* : a company of hired
musicians; Mercutio deliberately
mistakes Tybalt's meaning.
47   *fiddle-stick* : bow (in this case, his
sword).
48   *Zounds* : by God's wounds.
49   *haunt* : meeting place.

51   *coldly* : calmly.

addle as an egg for quarrelling. Thou hast quar-
25 relled with a man for coughing in the street,
because he hath wakened thy dog that hath lain
asleep in the sun. Didst thou not fall out with a
tailor for wearing his new doublet before Easter?
With another, for tying his new shoes with old rib-
30 and? And yet thou wilt tutor me from quarrelling
    Benvolio
And I were so apt to quarrel as thou art, any man
should buy the fee simple of my life for an hour and
a quarter.
    Mercutio
The fee simple! O simple!

         Enter Tybalt, *and Others*

    Benvolio
35 By my head, here comes the Capulets.
    Mercutio
By my heel, I care not.
    Tybalt
Follow me close, for I will speak to them.
Gentlemen, good e'en! A word with one of you.
    Mercutio
And but one word with one of us? Couple it with
40 something; make it a word and a blow.
    Tybalt
You shall find me apt enough to that, sir, and you
will give me occasion.
    Mercutio
Could you not take some occasion without giving?
    Tybalt
Mercutio, thou consort'st with Romeo—
    Mercutio
45 Consort! What, dost thou make us minstrels? And
thou make minstrels of us, look to hear nothing but
discords. Here's my fiddle-stick; here's that shall
make you dance. 'Zounds, consort!
    Benvolio
We talk here in the public haunt of men:
50 Either withdraw unto some private place,
Or reason coldly of your grievances,
Or else depart. Here all eyes gaze on us.

Mercutio
Men's eyes were made to look, and let them gaze;
I will not budge for no man's pleasure, I.

Enter Romeo

Tybalt
55 Well, peace be with you, sir. Here comes my man.
Mercutio
But I'll be hang'd, sir, if he wear your livery.
Marry, go before to field, he'll be your follower;
Your worship in that sense may call him 'man'.
Tybalt
Romeo, the love I bear thee can afford
60 No better term than this—thou art a villain.
Romeo
Tybalt, the reason that I have to love thee
Doth much excuse the appertaining rage
To such a greeting. Villain am I none.
Therefore farewell; I see thou know'st me not.
Tybalt
65 Boy, this shall not excuse the injuries
That thou hast done me. Therefore turn and draw.
Romeo
I do protest I never injur'd thee,
But love thee better than thou canst devise,
Till thou shalt know the reason of my love:
70 And so, good Capulet, which name I tender
As dearly as my own, be satisfied.
Mercutio
O calm, dishonourable, vile submission!
Alla stoccata carries it away.   [*Draws his sword*
Tybalt, you rat-catcher, will you walk?
Tybalt
75 What wouldst thou have with me?
Mercutio
Good King of Cats, nothing but one of your nine
lives, that I mean to make bold withal; and, as you
shall use me hereafter, dry-beat the rest of the
eight. Will you pluck your sword out of his pilcher
80 by the ears? Make haste, lest mine be about your
ears ere it be out.
Tybalt
[*Drawing his sword*] I am for you.

55   *my man :* Tybalt means 'the man I am looking for', but Mercutio again deliberately misunderstands him.
56   *livery :* uniform.
57   *go . . . follower :* if you lead the way to the battlefield, he will follow you.

60   *villain :* peasant (a great insult to a man of noble birth like Romeo).

62–3   *appertaining . . . greeting :* the anger that belongs (appertains) to such a greeting as 'Villain'.

68   *devise :* imagine.

70   *tender :* value.

73   *Alla stoccata :* at the thrust (an Italian fencing term). Mercutio uses it as a name for Tybalt.
        carries it away : has won.
74   *walk :* i.e. walk away, to fight a duel.
76   *King of Cats :* see note to *3, 4, 19*.
76–7   *nine lives :* in England, cats are (proverbially) said to have nine lives.
77   *make bold withal :* do as I please with.
78   *use me :* deal with me.
        dry-beat : beat without drawing blood.
79   *pilcher :* case.
80   *by the ears :* without ceremony.
80–1   *about your ears :* attacking you.

Romeo
Gentle Mercutio, put thy rapier up.
Mercutio
Come sir, your *passado*!   [*They fight*
Romeo
85 Draw, Benvolio! Beat down their weapons.
Gentlemen, for shame, forbear this outrage!
Tybalt, Mercutio, the Prince expressly hath
Forbid this bandying in Verona streets.
    Romeo *tries to stop the fighting,*
    but Tybalt *wounds* Mercutio

Hold, Tybalt! Good Mercutio!
            [*Exeunt* Tybalt *and his* Followers
Mercutio   I am hurt.
90 A plague o' both your houses! I am sped.
Is he gone, and hath nothing?
Benvolio   What, art thou hurt?
Mercutio
Ay, ay, a scratch, a scratch; marry, 'tis enough.
Where is my page? Go, villain, fetch a surgeon.
                            [*Exit* Page
Romeo
Courage, man; the hurt cannot be much.

84   *passado* : fencing thrust.

86   *forbear* : stop.

88   *bandying* : scuffling.

90.   *o'* : on.
      sped : killed.
91   *nothing* : i.e. no wound.

96 *serve :* i.e. to kill.

98 *peppered :* finished.

101 *book of arithmetic :* rule book.
102–3 *under your arm :* Mercutio believes that Romeo's intervention (in an attempt to stop the fighting) gave Tybalt opportunity to kill him.

107 *worms' meat :* a corpse.
  I have it : I have been wounded.
108 *soundly :* thoroughly (i.e. fatally).
  Your houses : Mercutio repeats his curse—'A plague o' both your houses'.
109 *ally :* kinsman.
110 *very :* true.
  mortal hurt : fatal wound.

115 *temper :* (a) character; (b) quality of steel.

117 *aspir'd :* ascended to.

119 *on . . . depend :* threatens more days.

123 *respective lenity :* mercy that has any respect (for his new kinship with Tybalt, or for the Prince's ruling).
124 *conduct :* guide.

Mercutio

95 No, 'tis not so deep as a well, nor so wide as a
church door; but 'tis enough, 'twill serve. Ask for
me tomorrow, and you shall find me a grave man. I
am peppered, I warrant, for this world. A plague o'
both your houses! 'Zounds, a dog, a rat, a mouse, a
100 cat, to scratch a man to death! A braggart, a rogue, a
villain, that fights by the book of arithmetic! Why
the devil came you between us? I was hurt under
your arm.

Romeo

I thought all for the best.

Mercutio

105 Help me into some house, Benvolio,
Or I shall faint. A plague o' both your houses!
They have made worms' meat of me: I have it,
And soundly too. Your houses!

[*Exeunt* Mercutio *and* Benvolio

Romeo

This gentleman, the Prince's near ally,
110 My very friend, hath got his mortal hurt
In my behalf; my reputation stain'd
With Tybalt's slander—Tybalt, that an hour
Hath been my cousin. O sweet Juliet!
Thy beauty hath made me effeminate,
115 And in my temper soften'd valour's steel!

Enter Benvolio

Benvolio

O Romeo, Romeo! Brave Mercutio is dead!
That gallant spirit hath aspir'd the clouds,
Which too untimely here did scorn the earth.

Romeo

This day's black fate on mo days doth depend;
120 This but begins the woe others must end.

Enter Tybalt

Benvolio

Here comes the furious Tybalt back again.

Romeo

Alive in triumph, and Mercutio slain!
Away to heaven, respective lenity,
And fire-ey'd fury be my conduct now!

126 *late :* recently.

128 *staying :* waiting.

130 *consort :* accompany.

133 *up :* aroused.
134 *doom thee :* condemn you to.

136 *fool :* plaything.

142 *discover :* reveal.
143 *manage :* course.

125 Now, Tybalt, take the 'villain' back again
That late thou gav'st me; for Mercutio's soul
Is but a little way above our heads,
Staying for thine to keep him company:
Either thou, or I, or both, must go with him.
        Tybalt
130 Thou wretched boy, that didst consort him here,
Shalt with him hence.
        Romeo   This shall determine that.
                        [*They fight :* Tybalt *falls*
        Benvolio
Romeo, away, be gone!
The citizens are up, and Tybalt slain.
Stand not amaz'd: the prince will doom thee death
135 If thou art taken: hence, be gone, away!
        Romeo
O, I am Fortune's fool.
        Benvolio   Why dost thou stay!
                        [*Exit* Romeo

                Enter Citizens

        Citizens
Which way ran he that kill'd Mercutio?
Tybalt, that murderer, which way ran he?
        Benvolio
There lies that Tybalt.
        1 Citizen   Up, sir, go with me.
140 I charge thee in the Prince's name, obey.

                Enter Prince Escalus, *attended;* Mon-
                tague, Capulet, *their* Wives *and Others.*
        Prince
Where are the vile beginners of this fray?
        Benvolio
O noble Prince, I can discover all
The unlucky manage of this fatal brawl.
There lies the man, slain by young Romeo,
145 That slew thy kinsman, brave Mercutio.
        Lady Capulet
Tybalt, my cousin! O my brother's child!
O prince! O cousin! Husband, O, the blood is
    spill'd
Of my dear kinsman. Prince, as thou art true,

For blood of ours shed blood of Montague.

150 O cousin, cousin!

Prince

Benvolio, who began this bloody fray!

Benvolio

Tybalt, here slain, whom Romeo's hand did slay.

Romeo, that spoke him fair, bade him bethink

How nice the quarrel was, and urg'd withal

155 Your high displeasure: all this, uttered

With gentle breath, calm look, knees humbly bow'd,

Could not take truce with the unruly spleen

Of Tybalt deaf to peace, but that he tilts

With piercing steel at bold Mercutio's breast;

160 Who, all as hot, turns deadly point to point,

And, with a martial scorn, with one hand beats

Cold death aside, and with the other sends

It back to Tybalt, whose dexterity

Retorts it. Romeo he cries aloud,

165 'Hold, friend! Friends, part!' and, swifter than his tongue,

His agile arm beats down their fatal points,

And 'twixt them rushes; underneath whose arm

An envious thrust from Tybalt hit the life

Of stout Mercutio, and then Tybalt fled;

170 But by and by comes back to Romeo,

Who had but newly entertain'd revenge,

And to 't they go like lightning; for, ere I

Could draw to part them, was stout Tybalt slain,

And, as he fell, did Romeo turn and fly.

175 This is the truth, or let Benvolio die.

Lady Capulet

He is a kinsman to the Montague;

Affection makes him false, he speaks not true.

Some twenty of them fought in this black strife,

And all those twenty could but kill one life.

180 I beg for justice, which thou, Prince, must give.

Romeo slew Tybalt: Romeo must not live.

Prince

Romeo slew him; he slew Mercutio.

Who now the price of his dear blood doth owe?

153 *spoke him fair :* spoke politely to him.

bethink : consider.

154 *nice :* trivial.

urg'd withal : argued in addition.

157 *take truce :* make peace.

spleen : temper.

158 *but that :* on the contrary.

tilts : thrusts.

160 *all as hot :* just as angry.

160–62 Probably Mercutio and Tybalt were fighting with both swords and daggers.

164 *Retorts it :* answers back.

168 *envious :* malicious.

hit the life : killed.

169 *stout :* brave.

171 *entertain'd :* thought about.

183 Who should pay the price of Mercutio's blood?

Montague

Not Romeo, Prince, he was Mercutio's friend;
185 His fault concludes but what the law should end,
The life of Tybalt.
            Prince   And for that offence
Immediately we do exile him hence.
I have an interest in your hate's proceeding,
My blood for your rude brawls doth lie a-bleeding.
190 But I'll amerce you with so strong a fine
That you shall all repent the loss of mine.
I will be deaf to pleading and excuses;
Nor tears nor prayers shall purchase out abuses.
Therefore use none. Let Romeo hence in haste,
195 Else, when he's found, that hour is his last.
Bear hence this body and attend our will:
Mercy but murders, pardoning those that kill.

                                        [*Exeunt*

188   *I have an interest :* I am
personally concerned.
        your hate's proceeding : the
progress of your hatred.
189   *blood :* kinsman.
190   *amèrce :* punish.
191   *loss of mine :* my loss.
193   *purchase out :* buy pardon for.

Act 3   Scene 2

Juliet is eagerly waiting for her
husband, but the Nurse brings bad
news.

1   *apace :* quickly.
        steeds : horses; they draw the
chariot of the classical sun-god,
Phoebus Apollo.
2   *lodging :* resting place.
3   *Phaeton :* the son of Phoebus
Apollo; he was allowed to drive his
father's chariot for one day, but he
drove too fast and was killed by
Jupiter.
5   *close :* i.e. providing secrecy.
        love-performing : suitable for
performing the act of love.
6   *runaway's eyes :* perhaps this
refers to the sun.
        wink : close, become blind.
9   *if love be blind :* see note to *1, 1,*
169 (and illustration, p. 10).
10   *best agrees with :* is most
appropriate for.
        civil : respectable.
12   *learn :* teach.
        lose a winning match : Juliet will
lose her virginity, but win a husband.

Scene 2 *Verona ; Capulet's house*

Enter Juliet

Juliet

Gallop apace, you fiery-footed steeds,
Towards Phœbus' lodging; such a waggoner
As Phaeton would whip you to the west,
And bring in cloudy night immediately.
5 Spread thy close curtain, love-performing night,
That runaway's eyes may wink, and Romeo
Leap to these arms, untalk'd of and unseen!
Lovers can see to do their amorous rites
By their own beauties; or, if love be blind,
10 It best agrees with night. Come, civil night,
Thou sober-suited matron, all in black,
And learn me how to lose a winning match,

14–15   *Hood ... mantle :* Juliet once
again uses the language of falconry (see
2, 2, 158ff); it is necessary to put a
hood over the head of a nervous hawk
which is fluttering its wings ('bating')
because it is unaccustomed to men
('unmanned').

15   *mantle :* cloak.
        strange : shy.

Play'd for a pair of stainless maidenhoods:
Hood my unmann'd blood, bating in my cheeks,

15 With thy black mantle; till strange love, grown
        bold,
Think true love acted simple modesty.
Come, night! Come, Romeo! Come, thou day in
        night;
For thou wilt lie upon the wings of night
Whiter than new snow on a raven's back.

20 Come, gentle night; come, loving, black-brow'd
        night,
Give me my Romeo. And when I shall die
Take him and cut him out in little stars,
And he will make the face of heaven so fine
That all the world will be in love with night,

25 And pay no worship to the garish sun.
O, I have bought the mansion of a love,
But not possess'd it; and, though I am sold,
Not yet enjoy'd. So tedious is this day
As is the night before some festival

30 To an impatient child that hath new robes
And may not wear them. O, here comes my Nurse,

27   *possess'd :* taken possession of.

Enter Nurse *with rope-ladder*

And she brings news; and every tongue that speaks
But Romeo's name speaks heavenly eloquence.
Now Nurse, what news? What, hast thou there the
        cords

35 That Romeo bade thee fetch?

33   *But :* only.
34   *cords :* rope-ladder.

Nurse   Ay, ay, the cords.
                                        [*Throws them down*
Juliet
Ah me! what news? Why dost thou wring thy
        hands?
Nurse
Ah well-a-day! He's dead, he's dead, he's dead!
We are undone, lady, we are undone!
Alack the day! He's gone, he's killed, he's dead!
Juliet

37   *well-a-day :* alas.
38   *undone :* ruined.

40 Can heaven be so envious?
Nurse   Romeo can,
Though heaven cannot. O Romeo, Romeo!
Who ever would have thought it? Romeo!

40   *envious :* spiteful.

Juliet
What devil art thou that dost torment me thus?
This torture should be roar'd in dismal hell.
45 Hath Romeo slain himself? Say thou but 'Ay',
And that bare vowel 'I' shall poison more
Than the death-darting eye of cockatrice.
I am not I, if there be such an 'I';
Or those eyes shut that makes thee answer 'Ay'.
50 If he be slain, say 'Ay'; or if not, 'No':
Brief sounds determine of my weal or woe.
    Nurse
I saw the wound, I saw it with mine eyes—
God save the mark!—here on his manly breast.
A piteous corse, a bloody piteous corse;
55 Pale, pale as ashes, all bedaub'd in blood,
All in gore blood; I swounded at the sight.
    Juliet
O break, my heart! Poor bankrupt, break at once!
To prison, eyes; ne'er look on liberty!
Vile earth, to earth resign; end motion here;
60 And thou and Romeo press one heavy bier!
    Nurse
O Tybalt, Tybalt! The best friend I had!
O courteous Tybalt, honest gentleman!
That ever I should live to see thee dead!
    Juliet
What storm is this that blows so contrary?
65 Is Romeo slaughter'd, and is Tybalt dead?
My dearest cousin, and my dearer lord?
Then, dreadful trumpet, sound the general doom!
For who is living if those two are gone?
    Nurse
Tybalt is gone, and Romeo banished;
70 Romeo that kill'd him, he is banished.
    Juliet
O God! Did Romeo's hand shed Tybalt's blood?
    Nurse
It did, it did! Alas the day, it did!
    Juliet
O serpent heart, hid with a flowering face!
Did ever dragon keep so fair a cave?
75 Beautiful tyrant! fiend angelical!
Dove-feather'd raven! wolvish-ravening lamb!

47   *cockatrice* : a fabulous serpent whose glance could kill.
49   *those eyes* : i.e. Romeo's eyes, closed in death.

51   *determine* : decide.
      weal : happiness.
52   *God save the mark* : forgive me for saying it.

54   *corse* : corpse.

56   *gore* : clotted.
      swounded : fainted.
57   *bankrupt* : Juliet feels that she has lost all her wealth.

59   *Vile earth* : vile body.
      to earth resign : yield to death.
      motion : movement, life.
60   *heavy* : sorrowful.

64   Juliet is confused.

67   *dreadful trumpet* : the one that will herald ('sound') the Day of Judgement ('general doom').

73   *serpent* : in some early pictures, the serpent (Satan) in the Garden of Eden appears as a face looking through flowers.
74   *keep* : hide in.
76   *wolvish-ravening* : ravenous as a wolf.

77   *show* : appearance.
78   *Just opposite* : the exact opposite.
justly seem'st : truly appeared.

81   *bower* : enclose.

87   *naught* : nothing.
88   *aqua vitae* : 'water of life'; a
modern equivalent is brandy.

98   *poor my lord* : my poor lord.
smooth : speak well of.

102 *native spring* : source—i.e. her
eyes.
103–4 Tears pay tribute, but the tribute
is due to sorrow; Juliet thinks that her
eyes have made a mistake and are
weeping for joy.

109 *forget it fain* : gladly forget it.
110 *presses* : pushes its way.

Despised substance of divinest show!
Just opposite to what thou justly seem'st;
A damned saint, an honourable villain!
80 O nature, what hadst thou to do in hell
When thou didst bower the spirit of a fiend
In mortal paradise of such sweet flesh?
Was ever book containing such vile matter
So fairly bound? O, that deceit should dwell
85 In such a gorgeous palace.
    Nurse   There's no trust,
No faith, no honesty in men; all perjured,
All forsworn, all naught, all dissemblers.
Ah, where's my man? Give me some *aqua vitae*.
These griefs, these woes, these sorrows make me
   old.
90 Shame come to Romeo!
    Juliet   Blister'd be thy tongue
For such a wish! He was not born to shame:
Upon his brow shame is asham'd to sit;
For 'tis a throne where honour may be crown'd
Sole monarch of the universal earth.
95 O what a beast was I to chide at him.
    Nurse
Will you speak well of him that kill'd your cousin?
    Juliet
Shall I speak ill of him that is my husband?
Ah, poor my lord, what tongue shall smooth thy
   name,
When I, thy three-hours wife, have mangl'd it?
100 But wherefore, villain, didst thou kill my cousin?
That villain cousin would have kill'd my husband.
Back, foolish tears, back to your native spring;
Your tributary drops belong to woe,
Which you, mistaking, offer up to joy.
105 My husband lives, that Tybalt would have slain;
And Tybalt's dead, that would have slain my
   husband:
All this is comfort. Wherefore weep I then?
Some word there was, worser than Tybalt's death,
That murder'd me: I would forget it fain;
110 But O, it presses to my memory
Like damned guilty deeds to sinners' minds.
'Tybalt is dead, and Romeo banished!'

That 'banished', that one word 'banished',
Hath slain ten thousand Tybalts. Tybalt's death

115 Was woe enough, if it had ended there;
Or, if sour woe delights in fellowship,
And needly will be rank'd with other griefs,
Why follow'd not, when she said 'Tybalt's dead',
Thy father, or thy mother—nay, or both,

120 Which modern lamentation might have mov'd?
But with a rearward following Tybalt's death,
'Romeo is banished!' To speak that word
Is father, mother, Tybalt, Romeo, Juliet,
All slain, all dead: 'Romeo is banished'!

125 There is no end, no limit, measure, bound
In that word's death; no words can that woe
      sound.
Where is my father and my mother, Nurse?

Nurse
Weeping and wailing over Tybalt's corse:
Will you go to them? I will bring you thither.

Juliet
130 Wash they his wounds with tears? Mine shall be
      spent,
When theirs are dry, for Romeo's banishment.
Take up those cords. Poor ropes, you are beguil'd,
Both you and I, for Romeo is exil'd:
He made you for a highway to my bed,

135 But I, a maid, die maiden-widowed.
Come, cords: come, Nurse. I'll to my wedding-bed;
And death, not Romeo, take my maidenhead!

Nurse
Hie to your chamber. I'll find Romeo
To comfort you: I wot well where he is.

140 Hark ye, your Romeo will be here at night.
I'll to him; he is hid at Laurence' cell.

Juliet
O, find him! Give this ring to my true knight.
And bid him come to take his last farewell.

                                          [*Exeunt*

116   *if . . . fellowship*: if one sorrow
   likes to have another for company.
117   *needly*: of necessity.
       rank'd: joined.

120   *modern*: ordinary.
       mov'd: caused.
121   *with a rearward following*:
   following, like a rearguard, the news of
   Tybalt's death.

126   *that word's death*: the death
   which that word brings.
       sound: express, measure.

130   *spent*: shed.

132   *beguil'd*: cheated.

135   *maid*: virgin.
       maiden-widowed: a virgin and a
   widow.

139   *wot*: know.

Act 3 Scene 3

Friar Laurence tries to console Romeo and to solve the dreadful problems that have arisen.

1 *fearful*: frightened.
2 *enamour'd of*: in love with.
  parts: nature, characters.

4 *doom*: judgement.
5 *craves*: desires.
  acquaintance at my hand: to be introduced to me.

8 *tidings*: news.

9 *doomsday*: the Day of Judgement (i.e. death).

10 *vanish'd*: issued.

13 *hath more terror in his look*: seems more terrifying.

17 *without*: outside.
19 *Hence banished*: to be banished from here (i.e. Verona).
20 *world's exile*: exile from the world.
21 *death mis-term'd*: the wrong name for what is in fact death.
21–2 *Calling . . . axe*: to speak of death as 'banishment' is like cutting off a man's head with a golden axe: it is still fatal.
25 *fault*: crime.
  calls: punishes with.
26 *rush'd*: swept.

Scene 3 *Verona: Friar Laurence's cell*

Enter Friar Laurence

Friar Laurence
Romeo, come forth; come forth thou fearful man.
Affliction is enamour'd of thy parts,
And thou art wedded to calamity.

Enter Romeo

Romeo
Father, what news? What is the Prince's doom?
5 What sorrow craves acquaintance at my hand,
That I yet know not?
Friar Laurence   Too familiar
Is my dear son with such sour company.
I bring thee tidings of the Prince's doom.
Romeo
What less than doomsday is the Prince's doom?
Friar Laurence
10 A gentler judgement vanish'd from his lips:
Not body's death, but body's banishment.
Romeo
Ha, banishment! Be merciful, say 'death'.
For exile hath more terror in his look,
Much more than death. Do not say 'banishment'.
Friar Laurence
15 Hence from Verona art thou banished.
Be patient, for the world is broad and wide.
Romeo
There is no world without Verona walls,
But purgatory, torture, hell itself.
Hence banished is banish'd from the world,
20 And world's exile is death; then 'banished'
Is death mis-term'd. Calling death 'banished'
Thou cutt'st my head off with a golden axe,
And smil'st upon the stroke that murders me.
Friar Laurence
O deadly sin! O rude unthankfulness!
25 Thy fault our law calls death; but the kind Prince,
Taking thy part, hath rush'd aside the law,
And turn'd that black word 'death' to banishment.
This is dear mercy, and thou seest it not.

Romeo
'Tis torture, and not mercy. Heaven is here,
30 Where Juliet lives; and every cat and dog
And little mouse, every unworthy thing,
Live here in heaven and may look on her.
But Romeo may not. More validity,
More honourable state, more courtship lives
35 In carrion flies than Romeo. They may seize
On the white wonder of dear Juliet's hand,
And steal immortal blessing from her lips,
Who, even in pure and vestal modesty,
Still blush, as thinking their own kisses sin.
40 But Romeo may not, he is banished.
Flies may do this, but I from this must fly
They are free men, but I am banished.
And sayest thou yet that exile is not death?
Hadst thou no poison mix'd, no sharp-ground
  knife,
45 No sudden mean of death, though ne'er so mean,
But 'banished' to kill me? 'Banished'!
O friar, the damned use that word in hell;
Howling attends it! How hast thou the heart,
Being a divine, a ghostly confessor,
50 A sin-absolver, and my friend profess'd,
To mangle me with that word 'banished'?
  Friar Laurence
Thou fond mad man, hear me a little speak.
  Romeo
O, thou wilt speak again of banishment.
  Friar Laurence
I'll give thee armour to keep off that word,
55 Adversity's sweet milk, philosophy,
To comfort thee, though thou art banished.
  Romeo
Yet 'banished'? Hang up philosophy!
Unless philosophy can make a Juliet,
Displant a town, reverse a prince's doom,
60 It helps not, it prevails not: talk no more.
  Friar Laurence
O, then I see that madmen have no ears.
  Romeo
How should they, when that wise men have no
  eyes?

33   *validity :* value.
34   *courtship :* courtly behaviour.
35   *carrion flies :* flies that feed on
dead flesh.

38   *vestal :* virgin.
39   *still blush :* are always blushing.
      as . . . sin : as if they think it is a
sin to touch each other.

44   *sharp-ground :* sharpened by
grinding.
45   *sudden mean of death :* quick way
to kill myself.
      ne'er so mean : however base.
48   *Howling attends it :* the anguished
cries of damned souls accompany the
word.
49   *a divine :* a priest.
      ghostly confessor : one who hears
the soul's confession.
50   *sin-absolver :* one who has the
power to forgive sins.
      my friend profess'd : one who
claims to be my friend.
51   *mangle :* wound, tear in pieces.
52   *fond :* foolish.

57   *Yet 'banished' :* do you still use
that word 'banished'?
      Hang up : throw away (unused
suits of armour were hung on the walls
of palaces).
59   *Displant :* transplant.
60   *prevails not :* is of no use.

63   *dispute with thee of thy estate :*
        discuss your condition with you.

66   *An hour but married :* married for
        no more than an hour.

70   *Taking the measure :* measuring
        the length.
70s.d. *within :* offstage.
71   *one :* someone.
72   *infold :* wrap itself round.

75   *taken :* captured.
        Stay awhile : wait a moment (the
        friar speaks to the person knocking).

77   *simpleness :* folly.

Friar Laurence
Let me dispute with thee of thy estate.
    Romeo
Thou canst not speak of that thou dost not feel.
65 Wert thou as young as I, Juliet thy love,
An hour but married, Tybalt murdered,
Doting like me, and like me banished,
Then mightst thou speak, then mightst thou tear
    thy hair,
And fall upon the ground, as I do now,
70 Taking the measure of an unmade grave.
                                    [*Knocking within*
    Friar Laurence
Arise; one knocks. Good Romeo, hide thyself.
    Romeo
Not I; unless the breath of heart-sick groans
Mist-like, infold me from the search of eyes.
                                    [*Knocking*
    Friar Laurence
Hark, how they knock! Who's there? Romeo, arise;
75 Thou wilt be taken.—Stay awhile!—Stand up;
                                    [*Knocking*
Run to my study.—By and by! God's will,
What simpleness is this! I come, I come!
                                    [*Knocking*
Who knocks so hard? Whence come you? What's
    your will?
    Nurse
[*Within*] Let me come in, and you shall know my
    errand:
80 I come from Lady Juliet.
    Friar Laurence
                                    Welcome, then.

                    Enter Nurse

    Nurse
O holy friar! O tell me, holy friar,
Where is my lady's lord, where's Romeo?
    Friar Laurence
There on the ground, with his own tears made
    drunk.

84   *even in my mistress' case :* in just
the same state as my mistress.

85   *woeful sympathy :* shared misery.

88   *and :* if

90   *so deep an O :* so profound a
lament.

92   *Spak'st :* did you speak?
How is it with her : how is she?
93   *old :* experienced.

95   *remov'd but little :* not very far
from.

97   *My conceal'd lady :* my secret
wife.

99   *starts :* jumps.

102   *level :* aim.

105   *anatomy :* body.
106   *lodge :* reside.
sack : ransack.
107   *mansion :* dwelling-place.
108   *cries out :* declares.
111–2 It is inappropriate for one who
looks like a man ('a seeming man') to
behave like a woman, and you are like
some monstrous ('ill-beseeming') beast
in appearing to be both man and
woman.
113   *my holy order :* the Order of St
Francis.
114   *temper'd :* disciplined.
116   *in thy life lives :* lives because you
live.
117   *doing damned hate :* by killing
himself, Romeo would commit a mortal
sin, leading to damnation.

Nurse
O, he is even in my mistress' case,
85 Just in her case! O woeful sympathy!
Piteous predicament! Even so lies she,
Blubbering and weeping, weeping and blubbering.
Stand up, stand up! Stand, and you be a man.
For Juliet's sake, for her sake, rise and stand;
90 Why should you fall into so deep an O?
        Romeo
Nurse!
        Nurse   Ah, sir! ah, sir! Death's the end of all.
        Romeo
Spak'st thou of Juliet? How is it with her?
Doth not she think me an old murderer,
Now I have stain'd the childhood of our joy
95 With blood remov'd but little from her own?
Where is she? and how doth she? and what says
My conceal'd lady to our cancell'd love?
        Nurse
O, she says nothing, sir, but weeps and weeps;
And now falls on her bed; and then starts up,
100 And Tybalt calls, and then on Romeo cries,
And then falls down again.
        Romeo   As if that name,
Shot from the deadly level of a gun,
Did murder her; as that name's cursed hand
Murder'd her kinsman. O tell me, friar, tell me,
105 In what vile part of this anatomy
Doth my name lodge? Tell me, that I may sack
The hateful mansion.   [*He draws his sword*
        Friar Laurence   Hold thy desperate hand:
Art thou a man? Thy form cries out thou art.
Thy tears are womanish; thy wild acts denote
110 The unreasonable fury of a beast:
Unseemly woman in a seeming man,
And ill-beseeming beast in seeming both!
Thou hast amaz'd me. By my holy order,
I thought thy disposition better temper'd.
115 Hast thou slain Tybalt? Wilt thou slay thyself?
And slay thy lady that in thy life lives,
By doing damned hate upon thyself?

118	*Why rail'st thou on*: why do you curse?

Why rail'st thou on thy birth, the heaven, and
    earth?
Since birth, and heaven, and earth, all three do
    meet
120 In thee at once, which thou at once wouldst lose.

121   *sham'st*: abuse.
    wit: intelligence.

Fie, fie, thou sham'st thy shape, thy love, thy wit,
Which, like a usurer, abound'st in all,
And usest none in that true use indeed
Which should bedeck thy shape, thy love, thy wit.

125 Thy noble shape is but a form of wax,

126   *Digressing*: departing.
127   *Thy dear love sworn*: the dear love which you have promised.
    hollow: empty.
128   *Killing*: because you kill.
130   *Misshapen*: misdirected.
    conduct: guidance (of his body and love).
129–33   Romeo's intelligence is like gunpowder carried (in a powder-flask) by an untrained soldier: in his ignorance he sets it alight, and is blown up ('dismember'd') by the very thing that should protect him.

Digressing from the valour of a man;
Thy dear love sworn but hollow perjury,
Killing that love which thou hast vow'd to cherish;
Thy wit, that ornament to shape and love,
130 Misshapen in the conduct of them both,
Like powder in a skill-less soldier's flask,
Is set a-fire by thine own ignorance,
And thou dismember'd with thine own defence.
What, rouse thee, man! Thy Juliet is alive,
135 For whose dear sake thou wast but lately dead;
There art thou happy. Tybalt would kill thee,
But thou slew'st Tybalt; there art thou happy.
The law that threaten'd death becomes thy friend,
And turns it to exile; there art thou happy.

140   *light*: alights.

140 A pack of blessings light upon thy back;
Happiness courts thee in her best array.
But, like a misbehav'd and sullen wench,
Thou pout'st upon thy fortune and thy love.
Take heed, take heed, for such die miserable.
145 Go, get thee to thy love, as was decreed,
Ascend her chamber—hence and comfort her;
But look thou stay not till the watch be set,

147   *watch*: guard (the police force that patrolled the city at night).
    set: in position.
148   *pass*: i.e. leave Verona.
150   *blaze*: announce.

For then thou canst not pass to Mantua,
Where thou shalt live till we can find a time
150 To blaze your marriage, reconcile your friends,
Beg pardon of the Prince, and call thee back
With twenty hundred thousand times more joy
Than thou went'st forth in lamentation.
Go before, Nurse. Commend me to thy lady,
155 And bid her hasten all the house to bed,

156   *apt unto*: ready for.

Which heavy sorrow makes them apt unto.
Romeo is coming.

Nurse

O Lord, I could have stay'd here all the night
To hear good counsel: O, what learning is.
160 My lord, I'll tell my lady you will come.

Romeo

Do so, and bid my sweet prepare to chide.

Nurse

Here, sir, a ring she bid me give you, sir.
Hie you, make haste, for it grows very late.   [*Exit*

Romeo

How well my comfort is reviv'd by this!

Friar Laurence

165 Go hence; good-night. And here stands all your
    state:
Either be gone before the watch be set,
Or by the break of day disguis'd from hence.
Sojourn in Mantua; I'll find out your man,
And he shall signify from time to time
170 Every good hap to you that chances here.
Give me thy hand. 'Tis late: farewell; good-night.

Romeo

But that a joy past joy calls out on me,
It were a grief so brief to part from thee.
Farewell.   [*Exeunt*

161   *chide*: scold me.

165   *here stands all your state*: your
    whole future depends on this.
166–7 Either leave before the evening
    watch is set, or go from Verona before
    dawn ('by the break of day').
168   *Sojourn*: stay.

170   *Every good hap*: every piece of
    good luck.

172   *calls out on me*: calls me away.
173   I would be sorry to leave you in
    such a hurry.

Act 3   Scene 4
Juliet's father makes plans for his
daughter's wedding to the County
Paris.

1   *fall'n out*: happened.
2   *move*: persuade (i.e. to marry
    Paris).

Scene 4 *Verona: Capulet's house*

Enter Capulet, Lady Capulet, *and* Paris

Capulet

Things have fall'n out, sir, so unluckily,
That we have had no time to move our daughter.
Look you, she lov'd her kinsman Tybalt dearly,
And so did I: well, we were born to die.
5 'Tis very late; she'll not come down to-night.
I promise you, but for your company,
I would have been a-bed an hour ago.

Paris

These times of woe afford no times to woo.
Madam, good-night. Commend me to your daugh-
    ter.

10   *know her mind* : know what she thinks (about the marriage).

11   *mew'd up to her heaviness* : shut up in her grief.

12   *tender* : offer.

Lady Capulet

10 I will, and know her mind early tomorrow.
   Tonight she's mew'd up to her heaviness.
      Capulet
   Sir Paris, I will make a desperate tender
   Of my child's love. I think she will be rul'd
   In all respects by me—nay, more, I doubt it not.
15 Wife, go you to her ere you go to bed;
   Acquaint her here of my son Paris' love;
   And bid her, mark you me, on Wednesday next—
   But, soft! what day is this?
      Paris   Monday, my lord.
      Capulet
   Monday! ha, ha! Well, Wednesday is too soon;
20 O' Thursday let it be—o' Thursday, tell her,
   She shall be married to this noble earl.
   Will you be ready? Do you like this haste?
   We'll keep no great ado—a friend or two;
   For, hark you, Tybalt being slain so late,

23   *keep no great ado* : have no grand affair.

24   *late* : recently.

25   *held him carelessly* : did not care very much about him.

25 It may be thought we held him carelessly,
   Being our kinsman, if we revel much.
   Therefore we'll have some half a dozen friends,
   And there an end. But what say you to Thursday?
      Paris
   My lord, I would that Thursday were tomorrow.
      Capulet

28   *there an end* : no more.

29   *I would* : I wish.

30 Well, get you gone: o' Thursday be it then.
   Go you to Juliet ere you go to bed;
   Prepare her, wife, against this wedding-day.
   Farewell, my lord. Light to my chamber, ho!
   Afore me! It is so very late,

32   *against* : in time for.

34   *Afore me* : indeed (a mild exclamation).

35 That we may call it early by and by.
   Good-night.   [*Exeunt*

Act 3   Scene 5

In Juliet's bedroom the two lovers say
goodbye; it is already dawn, and
Romeo must escape from Verona.
Their parting is interrupted by the
Nurse, giving warning that Juliet's
mother is looking for her daughter.
Lady Capulet brings news of the
wedding that has been arranged. Juliet
is horrified, and refuses to marry the
County Paris—much to her father's
anger.

3   *fearful*: full of fear.
4   *pomegranate*: pronounced (for
the rhythm) 'pom'granate'.
9   *Night's candles*: the stars.

13   *exhales*: the Elizabethans
believed that the sun draws up
('exhales') gases from the earth and sets
fire to them, producing shooting stars
(meteors).
17   *ta'en*: taken, caught.
18   *so*: if.
20   *reflex*: reflection.
Cynthia's brow: the moon;
Cynthia is another name for the
classical goddess of the moon.
21   *lark*: most birds sing when they
are perching, but the lark sings in
flight, when it is high in the air.
22   *vaulty*: arched (like a roof).
23   *care*: desire.
will: wish.
28   *straining*: uttering.
sharps: high, shrill notes of
music.
29   *division*: separation; in music,
this term describes a passage where
each note is sounded clearly and
sharply.
31   It was a popular belief that the
toad's fine eyes had once belonged to
the lark (whose eyes are ugly).
32   *I would*: I wish.
33   *arm from arm*: from each other.
affray: frighten.
34   *hunt's-up*: 'The hunt is up' was a
popular song of the time, calling
huntsmen to the field.

Scene 5 *Verona : Juliet's bedroom*

Enter Romeo *and* Juliet

Juliet
Wilt thou be gone? It is not yet near day:
It was the nightingale, and not the lark,
That pierc'd the fearful hollow of thine ear;
Nightly she sings on yon pomegranate tree:
5   Believe me, love, it was the nightingale.
Romeo
It was the lark, the herald of the morn,
No nightingale. Look, love, what envious streaks
Do lace the severing clouds in yonder east.
Night's candles are burnt out, and jocund day
10   Stands tiptoe on the misty mountain tops.
I must be gone and live, or stay and die.
Juliet
Yon light is not daylight, I know it, I.
It is some meteor that the sun exhales
To be to thee this night a torch-bearer,
15   And light thee on thy way to Mantua.
Therefore stay yet; thou need'st not to be gone.
Romeo
Let me be ta'en, let me be put to death;
I am content, so thou wilt have it so.
I'll say yon grey is not the morning's eye,
20   'Tis but the pale reflex of Cynthia's brow;
Nor that is not the lark, whose notes do beat
The vaulty heaven so high above our heads:
I have more care to stay than will to go.
Come, death, and welcome! Juliet wills it so.
25   How is 't, my soul? Let's talk; it is not day.
Juliet
It is, it is! Hie hence, be gone, away!
It is the lark that sings so out of tune,
Straining harsh discords and unpleasing sharps.
Some say the lark makes sweet division;
30   This doth not so, for she divideth us.
Some say the lark and loathed toad change eyes;
O now I would they had chang'd voices too,
Since arm from arm that voice doth us affray,
Hunting thee hence with hunt's-up to the day.
35   O now be gone; more light and light it grows.

Romeo
More light and light; more dark and dark our woes.

Enter Nurse

Nurse
Madam!
Juliet
Nurse?
Nurse
Your lady mother is coming to your chamber.

40 The day is broke; be wary, look about   [*Exit*
Juliet
Then, window, let day in, and let life out.
Romeo
Farewell, farewell! One kiss, and I'll descend.
[*Descends*
Juliet
Art thou gone so? Love, lord, ay husband, friend!
I must hear from thee every day in the hour,
45 For in a minute there are many days:
O by this count I shall be much in years
Ere I again behold my Romeo.
Romeo
Farewell!
I will omit no opportunity
50 That may convey my greetings, love, to thee.
Juliet
O, think'st thou we shall ever meet again?
Romeo
I doubt it not; and all these woes shall serve
For sweet discourses in our times to come.
Juliet
O God! I have an ill-divining soul:
55 Methinks I see thee, now thou art so low,
As one dead in the bottom of a tomb:
Either my eyesight fails, or thou look'st pale.
Romeo
And trust me, love, in my eye so do you:
Dry sorrow drinks our blood. Adieu, adieu!
[*Exit*
Juliet
60 O Fortune, Fortune! All men call thee fickle:
If thou art fickle, what dost thou with him

40   *look about :* watch out.

44–5   Juliet fancies that there are whole days in hours and even in minutes (as well as minutes in hours and hours in days).
46   *count :* way of reckoning.
        much in years : very old.

54   *ill-divining :* prophesying evil.
55   *so low :* i.e. because he has climbed down from the balcony.

59   *Dry :* thirsty; every sigh (the Elizabethans believed) wasted a drop of blood.

That is renown'd for faith? Be fickle, Fortune;
For then, I hope, thou wilt not keep him long,
But send him back.

Lady Capulet

[*Within*] Ho, daughter! Are you up?

Juliet

65 Who is't that calls? It is my lady mother!
Is she not down so late, or up so early?
What unaccustom'd cause procures her hither?

Enter Lady Capulet

Lady Capulet

Why, how now, Juliet?

Juliet   Madam, I am not well.

Lady Capulet

Evermore weeping for your cousin's death?
70 What, wilt thou wash him from his grave with
    tears?
And if thou couldst, thou couldst not make him live;
Therefore, have done. Some grief shows much of
    love;
But much of grief shows still some want of wit.

Juliet

Yet let me weep for such a feeling loss.

Lady Capulet

75 So shall you feel the loss, but not the friend
Which you weep for.

Juliet   Feeling so the loss,
I cannot choose but ever weep the friend.

Lady Capulet

Well, girl, thou weep'st not so much for his death,
As that the villain lives which slaughter'd him.

Juliet

80 What villain, madam?

Lady Capulet   That same villain, Romeo.

Juliet

[*Aside*] Villain and he be many miles asunder.
God pardon him! I do, with all my heart;
And yet no man like he doth grieve my heart.

Lady Capulet

That is because the traitor murderer lives.

66 Is she very late in going to bed,
or very early in getting up?
67 *procures*: brings.

68 *how now*: what is the matter?

72 *have done*: stop (i.e. crying).
some . . . love: moderate grief
shows great love.
73 But a lot of grief always shows
lack of commonsense.
74 *such a feeling loss*: a loss that I
feel so much.
75 By weeping, Juliet will feel the
loss of Tybalt, but she will not be able
to bring him back to life so that she can
touch (i.e. feel) him.

81 Romeo is very far from being a
villain.

Juliet

85 Ay, madam, from the reach of these my hands.
Would none but I might venge my cousin's death!

Lady Capulet

We will have vengeance for it, fear thou not.
Then weep no more. I'll send to one in Mantua,
Where that same banish'd runagate doth live,
90 Shall give him such an unaccustom'd dram
That he shall soon keep Tybalt company:
And then, I hope, thou wilt be satisfied.

Juliet

Indeed, I never shall be satisfied
With Romeo, till I behold him—dead—
95 Is my poor heart so for a kinsman vex'd.
Madam, if you could find out but a man
To bear a poison, I would temper it,
That Romeo should, upon receipt thereof,
Soon sleep in quiet. O, how my heart abhors
100 To hear him nam'd, and cannot come to him,
To wreak the love I bore my cousin Tybalt
Upon his body that hath slaughter'd him.

Lady Capulet

Find thou the means, and I'll find such a man.
But now I'll tell thee joyful tidings, girl.

Juliet

105 And joy comes well in such a needy time:
What are they, I beseech your ladyship?

Lady Capulet

Well, well, thou hast a careful father, child;
One who, to put thee from thy heaviness,
Hath sorted out a sudden day of joy
110 That thou expect'st not, nor I look'd not for.

Juliet

Madam, in happy time! What day is that?

Lady Capulet

Marry, my child, early next Thursday morn
The gallant, young, and noble gentleman,
The County Paris, at Saint Peter's church,
115 Shall happily make thee there a joyful bride.

Juliet

Now, by Saint Peter's church, and Peter too,
He shall not make me there a joyful bride!
I wonder at this haste; that I must wed

---

86   I wish that no one except I might have the power to avenge ('venge') Tybalt's death.

88   *one :* someone I know.
89   *runagate :* wretch, law-breaker.
90   *unaccustom'd :* unusual.
      dram : little drink.

95   *vex'd :* troubled.
96   *find out but :* only find out.
97   *temper :* mix.

101 *wreak :* express.

105 *needy :* unhappy.

107 *careful :* caring.
108 *heaviness :* sorrow.
109 *sorted out :* selected.
      sudden : surprising.
110 *look'd not for :* did not expect.

111 *in happy time :* how fortunate.

Ere he that should be husband comes to woo.
120 I pray you, tell my lord and father, madam,
I will not marry yet; and, when I do, I swear,
It shall be Romeo, whom you know I hate,
Rather than Paris. These are news indeed!

Lady Capulet
Here comes your father; tell him so yourself,
125 And see how he will take it at your hands.

Enter Capulet *and* Nurse

Capulet
When the sun sets, the air doth drizzle dew;
But for the sunset of my brother's son
It rains downright.

129 *conduit :* water-pipe.

How now! A conduit, girl? What, still in tears?
130 Evermore showering? In one little body

131 *counterfeit'st :* imitate.
bark : boat.

Thou counterfeit'st a bark, a sea, a wind;
For still thy eyes, which I may call the sea,
Do ebb and flow with tears; the bark thy body is,
Sailing in this salt flood; the winds thy sighs
135 Who, raging with thy tears, and they with them,

136 *Without :* unless there is.

Without a sudden calm, will overset
Thy tempest-tossed body. How now, wife?

138 *decree :* decision.

Have you deliver'd to her our decree?

Lady Capulet

139 *will none :* will not hear of it.

Ay, sir; but she will none, she gives you thanks.
140 I would the fool were married to her grave!

Capulet

141 *Take me with you :* let me understand you.

Soft! Take me with you, take me with you, wife.
How? Will she none? Doth she not give us thanks?
Is she not proud? doth she not count her bless'd,

144 *wrought :* persuaded.
145 *bride :* bridegroom (in the sixteenth century the word could be used for either partner).

Unworthy as she is, that we have wrought
145 So worthy a gentleman to be her bride?

Juliet

148 *meant love :* intended as love.
149 *chop-logic :* one who engages in verbal battles.

Not proud you have; but thankful that you have.
Proud can I never be of what I hate;
But thankful even for hate that is meant love.

Capulet

151 *minion :* minx.
152 Capulet tells his daughter not to use the word 'thanks' or the word 'proud' in his presence.

How now, how now? chop-logic! What is this?
150 'Proud', and 'I thank you', and 'I thank you not';
And yet 'not proud'? Mistress minion, you,

153 *fettle your fine joints :* prepare yourself (the phrase would be used to a groom, with reference to his horses).
'gainst : ready for.

Thank me no thankings, nor proud me no prouds,
But fettle your fine joints 'gainst Thursday next,

155	*hurdle* : wooden rack—used for dragging traitors to the place of execution.
156	*green-sickness* : anaemic.
157	*tallow-face* : Juliet's grief has made her face waxen (pale).

To go with Paris to Saint Peter's church,
155 Or I will drag thee on a hurdle thither.
Out, you green-sickness carrion! Out, you bag-
      gage!
You tallow-face!

Lady Capulet Fie, fie! What, are you mad?

Juliet
Good father, I beseech you on my knees,
Hear me with patience but to speak a word.

Capulet
160 Hang thee, young baggage! Disobedient wretch!
I tell thee what, get thee to church o' Thursday,
Or never after look me in the face.
Speak not, reply not, do not answer me;

164	*itch* : i.e. to strike his daughter.

My fingers itch. Wife, we scarce thought us bless'd
165 That God had lent us but this only child;
But now I see this one is one too much,
And that we have a curse in having her.
Out on her, hilding!

168	*hilding* : worthless creature.

Nurse   God in heaven bless her!
You are to blame, my lord, to rate her so.

169	*rate* : scold.

Capulet
170 And why, my Lady Wisdom? Hold your tongue,
Good Prudence; smatter with your gossips, go.

171	*smatter* : chatter. *gossips* : old women.

Nurse
I speak no treason.

Capulet   O, God ye good e'en.

Nurse
May not one speak?

Capulet   Peace, you mumbling fool!
Utter your gravity o'er a gossip's bowl;

174	*gravity* : words of wisdom.
175	*hot* : angry.

175 For here we need it not.

Lady Capulet   You are too hot.

Capulet

176	*God's bread* : i.e. the bread consecrated at the mass.

God's bread! It makes me mad.
Day, night, hour, tide, time, work, play,
Alone, in company—still my care hath been

178	*still* : always.
179	*match'd* : suitably married.

To have her match'd. And having now provided
180 A gentleman of noble parentage,

181	*demesnes* : property. *lin'd* : descended.
182	*parts* : qualities.
183	*Proportion'd* : shaped.
184	*puling* : whimpering.

Of fair demesnes, youthful, and nobly lin'd
Stuff'd, as they say, with honourable parts,
Proportion'd as one's thought would wish a man—
And then to have a wretched puling fool,

185   *whining mammet* : crying doll.
    in her fortune's tender : when her good luck is offered to her.

189   *house* : live.
190   *do not use to* : am not accustomed to.
191   *Lay hand on heart* : think honestly.
    advise : consider.

196   *be forsworn* : break my word.

202   *monument* : tomb.

206   Juliet's marriage vow is registered in heaven, and so long as Romeo is alive, she cannot be released from it.

210   *practise stratagems* : play cruel tricks.

214   *all the world to nothing* : the Nurse is willing to lay this bet.
215   *challenge you* : claim you (as his wife).

220   *a dishclout to him* : a dishcloth compared to Paris.

---

185 A whining mammet, in her fortune's tender,
To answer 'I'll not wed, I cannot love,
I am too young, I pray you pardon me'.
But, and you will not wed, I'll pardon you:
Graze where you will, you shall not house with me.
190 Look to 't, think on 't; I do not use to jest.
Thursday is near. Lay hand on heart; advise.
And you be mine, I'll give you to my friend;
And you be not, hang, beg, starve, die in the streets,
For, by my soul, I'll ne'er acknowledge thee,
195 Nor what is mine shall never do thee good.
Trust to 't, bethink you. I'll not be forsworn.
                                [*Exit*

    Juliet
Is there no pity sitting in the clouds,
That sees into the bottom of my grief?
O sweet my mother, cast me not away!
200 Delay this marriage for a month, a week;
Or, if you do not, make the bridal bed
In that dim monument where Tybalt lies.
        Lady Capulet
Talk not to me, for I'll not speak a word.
Do as thou wilt, for I have done with thee.   [*Exit*
        Juliet
205 O God—O Nurse, how shall this be prevented?
My husband is on earth, my faith in heaven;
How shall that faith return again to earth,
Unless that husband sent it me from heaven
By leaving earth? Comfort me, counsel me.
210 Alack, alack! That heaven should practise stra-
    tagems
Upon so soft a subject as myself!
What sayst thou? Hast thou not a word of joy?
Some comfort, Nurse?
        Nurse   Faith, here it is. Romeo
Is banished; and all the world to nothing
215 That he dares ne'er come back to challenge you;
Or, if he do, it needs must be by stealth.
Then, since the case so stands as now it doth,
I think it best you married with the County.
O, he's a lovely gentleman!
220 Romeo's a dishclout to him. An eagle, madam,
Hath not so green, so quick, so fair an eye

222   *Beshrew my very heart :* curse my
heart, indeed.
223   *happy :* fortunate.

228   *Amen :* Juliet endorses the Nurse's
curse on her heart and soul.

234   *Ancient damnation :* damned old
woman.
235   *sin :* sinful.
237   *above compare :* as being above
comparison.
239   *twain :* two (i.e. Juliet will no
longer confide in her Nurse).
240   *I'll to :* I'll go to.
241   *myself have power to die :* it is in
my own power to kill myself.

As Paris hath. Beshrew my very heart,
I think you are happy in this second match,
For it excels your first: or if it did not,
225 Your first is dead—or 'twere as good he were,
As living here and you no use of him.
        Juliet
Speak'st thou from thy heart?
        Nurse   And from my soul too;
Or else beshrew them both.
        Juliet   Amen!
        Nurse   What!
        Juliet
Well, thou hast comforted me marvellous much.
230 Go in; and tell my lady I am gone,
Having displeas'd my father, to Laurence' cell,
To make confession and to be absolv'd.
        Nurse
Marry, I will; and this is wisely done.   [*Exit*
        Juliet
Ancient damnation! O most wicked fiend!
235 Is it more sin to wish me thus forsworn,
Or to dispraise my lord with that same tongue
Which she hath prais'd him with above compare
So many thousand times? Go, counsellor!
Thou and my bosom henceforth shall be twain.
240 I'll to the friar, to know his remedy:
If all else fail, myself have power to die.   [*Exit*

Act 4

3   *I am nothing slow* : I do not want
to be slow.
       slack : lessen.
4   *mind* : opinion.
5   *Uneven* : irregular.
       course : procedure.

8   *Venus* : Roman goddess of love.

10   *sway* : scope.

12   *inundation* : flooding.
13   *minded* : thought about.

Scene 1 *Verona : Friar Laurence's cell*

Enter Friar Laurence *and* Paris

Friar Laurence
On Thursday, sir? The time is very short.
     Paris
My father Capulet will have it so,
And I am nothing slow to slack his haste.
     Friar Laurence
You say you do not know the lady's mind.
5 Uneven is the course, I like it not.
     Paris
Immoderately she weeps for Tybalt's death,
And therefore have I little talk of love;
For Venus smiles not in a house of tears.
Now, sir, her father counts it dangerous
10 That she doth give her sorrow so much sway.
And in his wisdom hastes our marriage
To stop the inundation of her tears;
Which, too much minded by herself alone,
May be put from her by society.
15 Now do you know the reason of this haste.
     Friar Laurence
[*Aside*] I would I knew not why it should be
     slow'd.
Look, sir, here comes the lady toward my cell.

Enter Juliet

     Paris
Happily met, my lady and my wife!
     Juliet
That may be, sir, when I may be a wife.
     Paris
20 That 'may be' must be, love, on Thursday next.

21   *a certain text :* a true saying.

Juliet

What must be shall be.

Friar Laurence   That's a certain text.

Paris

Come you to make confession to this father?

Juliet

To answer that, I should confess to you.

Paris

Do not deny to him that you love me.

Juliet

25 I will confess to you that I love him.

Paris

So will ye, I am sure, that you love me.

Juliet

If I do so, it will be of more price,

Being spoke behind your back, than to your face.

Paris

Poor soul, thy face is much abus'd with tears.

Juliet

30 The tears have got small victory by that;

For it was bad enough before their spite.

Paris

Thou wrong'st it, more than tears, with that report.

Juliet

That is no slander, sir, which is a truth;

And what I spake, I spake it to my face.

Paris

35 Thy face is mine, and thou hast slander'd it.

Juliet

It may be so, for it is not mine own.

Are you at leisure, holy father, now;

Or shall I come to you at evening mass?

Friar Laurence

My leisure serves me, pensive daughter, now.

39   *my leisure serves me :* I am free.

40   *entreat the time alone :* ask to be
alone for the present.

41   *shield :* forbid.

42   *will I rouse ye :* the Elizabethan
wedding-day started when the
bridegroom, accompanied by
musicians, came to the girl's house in
the early morning and led his bride
from her bedroom to the church.

40 My lord, we must entreat the time alone.

Paris

God shield I should disturb devotion!

Juliet, on Thursday early will I rouse ye:

Till then, adieu; and keep this holy kiss.   [*Exit*

Juliet

O, shut the door! and when thou hast done so,

45 Come weep with me. Past hope, past care, past
help!

47   *strains* : perplexes.
      compass of my wits : limits of my
mind.
48   *prorogue* : postpone.

53   *resolution* : decision.
54   *presently* : immediately.

57   *label* : the wax seal fastened to a
document ('deed') to make it legal.

59   *both* : i.e. her hand and her heart.
60   *long-experienc'd time* : age and
experience.
61   *present counsel* : advice at once.
62   *extremes* : sufferings.
63   *arbitrating that* : resolving that
problem.
64   *commission* : authority.
      art : skill.
65   *issue of true honour* : honourable
solution.
66   *Be not so long to speak* : say
something quickly.
69–70 Which is as dangerous to put
into practice as the danger we are
trying to prevent.

74   *chide* : drive.
75   Since you struggle ('cop'st') with
death himself to escape from the
shame.

79   *thievish ways* : dens of thieves.
      lurk : linger.

Friar Laurence
O Juliet, I already know thy grief;
It strains me past the compass of my wits.
I hear thou must, and nothing may prorogue it,
On Thursday next be married to this County.
    Juliet
50 Tell me not, friar, that thou hear'st of this,
Unless thou tell me how I may prevent it.
If, in thy wisdom, thou canst give no help,
Do thou but call my resolution wise,
And with this knife I'll help it presently.
55 God join'd my heart and Romeo's, thou our hands;
And ere this hand, by thee to Romeo's seal'd,
Shall be the label to another deed,
Or my true heart with treacherous revolt
Turn to another, this shall slay them both.
60 Therefore, out of thy long-experienc'd time,
Give me some present counsel; or behold,
'Twixt my extremes and me this bloody knife
Shall play the umpire, arbitrating that
Which the commission of thy years and art
65 Could to no issue of true honour bring.
Be not so long to speak; I long to die,
If what thou speak'st speak not of remedy.
    Friar Laurence
Hold, daughter; I do spy a kind of hope,
Which craves as desperate an execution
70 As that is desperate which we would prevent.
If, rather than to marry County Paris,
Thou hast the strength of will to slay thyself,
Then is it likely thou wilt undertake
A thing like death to chide away this shame,
75 That cop'st with death himself to 'scape from it;
And, if thou dar'st, I'll give thee remedy.
    Juliet
O bid me leap, rather than marry Paris,
From off the battlements of any tower,
Or walk in thievish ways, or bid me lurk
80 Where serpents are; chain me with roaring bears,

81 *charnel-house :* the repository for bones dug up in the course of digging new graves in the churchyard.
83 *reeky :* stinking.
    chapless : jaw-less (the bottom of the jaw would be knocked off with the spade).

91 *look :* see to it.
    lie : sleep
93 *vial :* small bottle.
95 *presently :* at once.
96 *a cold and drowsy humour :* a fluid which will make you cold and drowsy.
97 *native progress :* natural movement.
    surcease : stop.
100 *to wanny ashes :* to become as pale as ashes.
    eyes' windows : eyelids.
102 *supple government :* power of movement.
104 *borrow'd :* false.
109 *manner :* fashion.

Or hide me nightly in a charnel-house,
O'er-cover'd quite with dead men's rattling bones,
With reeky shanks, and yellow chapless skulls;
Or bid me go into a new-made grave
85 And hide me with a dead man in his shroud—
Things that, to hear them told, have made me tremble—
And I will do it without fear or doubt,
To live an unstain'd wife to my sweet love.

Friar Laurence
Hold, then. Go home, be merry, give consent
90 To marry Paris. Wednesday is tomorrow:
Tomorrow night look that thou lie alone,
Let not thy Nurse lie with thee in thy chamber.
Take thou this vial, being then in bed,
And this distilled liquor drink thou off;
95 When presently through all thy veins shall run
A cold and drowsy humour, for no pulse
Shall keep his native progress, but surcease.
No warmth, no breath, shall testify thou liv'st;
The roses in thy lips and cheeks shall fade
100 To wanny ashes; thy eyes' windows fall,
Like death when he shuts up the day of life.
Each part, depriv'd of supple government,
Shall, stiff and stark and cold, appear like death;
And in this borrow'd likeness of shrunk death
105 Thou shalt continue two-and-forty hours,
And then awake as from a pleasant sleep.
Now, when the bridegroom in the morning comes
To rouse thee from thy bed, there art thou—dead.
Then, as the manner of our country is,

110   *uncovered* : with face uncovered (probably because—in the eyes of society—she was not married).

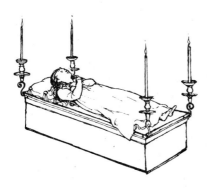

113   *against* : ready for.
114   *drift* : plan.
119   *inconstant toy* : irresolute fancy.
120   *Abate* : weaken.
122   *Hold* : here it is.
125   *help afford* : give help.

110   In thy best robes uncover'd on the bier,
       Thou shalt be borne to that same ancient vault
       Where all the kindred of the Capulets lie.
       In the meantime, against thou shalt awake,
       Shall Romeo by my letters know our drift,
115   And hither shall he come; and he and I
       Will watch thy waking, and that very night
       Shall Romeo bear thee hence to Mantua.
       And this shall free thee from this present shame,
       If no inconstant toy nor womanish fear
120   Abate thy valour in the acting it.
           Juliet
       Give me, give me! O tell me not of fear!
           Friar Laurence
       Hold. Get you gone. Be strong and prosperous
       In this resolve. I'll send a friar with speed
       To Mantua, with my letters to thy lord.
           Juliet
125   Love, give me strength, and strength shall help
           afford.
       Farewell, dear father!   [*Exeunt*

Act 4   Scene 2
The Capulets are preparing for the wedding. Juliet assures her father that she will be obedient.

1   *writ* : written.

2   *cunning* : skilful.

3   *none ill* : no bad ones.
       try : test.

10   *unfurnish'd* : unprepared.

Scene 2 *Verona : Capulet's house*

           Enter Capulet, Lady Capulet, Nurse,
           and Servants

           Capulet
       So many guests invite as here are writ.
                                    [*Exit* 1 Servant
       Sirrah, go hire me twenty cunning cooks.
           2 Servant
       You shall have none ill, sir; for I'll try if they can
       lick their fingers.
           Capulet
5   How canst thou try them so?
           2 Servant
       Marry, sir, 'tis an ill cook that cannot lick his own
       fingers: therefore he that cannot lick his fingers
       goes not with me.
           Capulet
       Go, be gone.   [*Exit* 2 Servant
10   We shall be much unfurnish'd for this time.

What, is my daughter gone to Friar Laurence?
> **Nurse**
> Ay, forsooth.
> **Capulet**
> Well, he may chance to do some good on her:
> A peevish self-will'd harlotry it is.
> **Nurse**

14 *harlotry :* worthless creature.

15 *shrift :* confession.

15 See where she comes from shrift with merry look.

Enter Juliet

> **Capulet**

16 *headstrong :* stubborn one.

How now, my headstrong! Where have you been
    gadding?
> **Juliet**
> Where I have learn'd me to repent the sin
> Of disobedient opposition

19 *behests :* demands.
   enjoin'd : instructed.

To you and your behests; and am enjoin'd
20 By holy Laurence to fall prostrate here,
And beg your pardon. Pardon, I beseech you!

22 *I am ever rul'd :* I always will be
ruled.

Henceforward I am ever rul'd by you.
> **Capulet**
> Send for the County; go tell him of this:
> I'll have this knot knit up tomorrow morning.

24 *knot :* i.e. the marriage tie.

> **Juliet**

26 *becomed :* appropriate.

25 I met the youthful lord at Laurence' cell,
And gave him what becomed love I might,
Not stepping o'er the bounds of modesty.
> **Capulet**
> Why, I am glad on 't; this is well. Stand up:
> This is as 't should be. Let me see the County.
> 30 Ay, marry, go, I say, and fetch him hither.
> Now, afore God, this reverend holy friar,
> All our whole city is much bound to him.
> **Juliet**
> Nurse, will you go with me into my closet,
> To help me sort such needful ornaments

34 *sort :* choose.
35 *furnish :* equip.

35 As you think fit to furnish me to-morrow?
> **Lady Capulet**
> No, not till Thursday; there is time enough.
> **Capulet**
> Go, Nurse, go with her. We'll to church tomorrow.
>   [*Exeunt* Juliet *and* Nurse

38   *short in our provision :* not have enough food ready.

Lady Capulet
We shall be short in our provision:
'Tis now near night.
    Capulet   Tush! I will stir about,
40 And all things shall be well, I warrant thee, wife.
    Go thou to Juliet, help to deck up her.
    I'll not to bed tonight. Let me alone;
    I'll play the housewife for this once. What, ho!
    They are all forth. Well, I will walk myself
45 To County Paris, to prepare up him
    Against tomorrow. My heart is wondrous light,
    Since this same wayward girl is so reclaim'd.
                                        [*Exeunt*

41   *deck up :* dress up.
42   *Let me alone :* leave it to me.

44   *forth :* out.

46   *Against :* ready for.
47   *reclaim'd :* brought back to obedience.

Act 4   Scene 3
Juliet prepares to take the friar's drug.

Scene 3 *Verona : Juliet's bedroom*

Enter Juliet *and* Nurse

Juliet
Ay, those attires are best; but, gentle Nurse,
I pray thee, leave me to myself tonight;
For I have need of many orisons
To move the heavens to smile upon my state,
5 Which, well thou know'st, is cross and full of sin.

1   *attires :* clothes.

3   *orisons :* prayers.

5   *cross :* stubborn.

Enter Lady Capulet

Lady Capulet
What, are you busy, ho? Need you my help?
Juliet
No, madam; we have cull'd such necessaries
As are behoveful for our state tomorrow:
So please you, let me now be left alone,
10 And let the Nurse this night sit up with you;
For, I am sure, you have your hands full all
In this so sudden business.
    Lady Capulet   Good-night:
Get thee to bed, and rest; for thou hast need.
                    [*Exeunt* Lady Capulet *and* Nurse
Juliet
Farewell! God knows when we shall meet again.
15 I have a faint cold fear thrills through my veins,
That almost freezes up the heat of life.

7   *cull'd :* picked out.
8   *behoveful :* needful.

15   *faint cold fear :* fear which causes faintness and cold.
      thrills : trembles.

I'll call them back again to comfort me:
Nurse!—What should she do here?
My dismal scene I needs must act alone.
20 Come, vial.
What if this mixture do not work at all?
Shall I be married then tomorrow morning?
No, no; this shall forbid it: lie thou there.

[*Laying down a dagger*

What if it be a poison, which the friar
25 Subtly hath minister'd to have me dead,
Lest in this marriage he should be dishonour'd
Because he married me before to Romeo?
I fear it is: and yet, methinks, it should not,
For he hath still been tried a holy man.
30 How if, when I am laid into the tomb,
I wake before the time that Romeo
Come to redeem me? There's a fearful point!
Shall I not then be stifled in the vault,
To whose foul mouth no healthsome air breathes
    in,
35 And there die strangl'd ere my Romeo comes?
Or, if I live, is it not very like,
The horrible conceit of death and night,
Together with the terror of the place—
As in a vault, an ancient receptacle,
40 Where for these many hundred years the bones
Of all my buried ancestors are pack'd;
Where bloody Tybalt, yet but green in earth,
Lies festering in his shroud; where, as they say,
At some hours in the night spirits resort!
45 Alack, alack, is it not like that I,
So early waking, what with loathsome smells,
And shrieks like mandrakes torn out of the earth,
That living mortals, hearing them, run mad:
O, if I wake, shall I not be distraught,
50 Environed with all these hideous fears,
And madly play with my forefathers' joints,
And pluck the mangled Tybalt from his shroud?
And, in this rage, with some great kinsman's bone,
As with a club, dash out my desperate brains?
55 O look! Methinks I see my cousin's ghost

19   *dismal* : dreadful.

23   *this* : i.e. the dagger.

25   *Subtly* : cunningly, deceitfully.
      minister'd : provided, prescribed.

29   *still been tried* : always been
   found.

32   *redeem* : rescue.

34   *healthsome* : wholesome, healthy.

37   *conceit of* : thoughts produced by.

42   *yet* : still.
      but green in earth : just recently
   dead.

47   *mandrakes* : plants whose forked
   roots gave them the rough shape of a
   man. Popular superstition said that the
   mandrake screamed when it was pulled
   out of the earth and humans who heard
   the screams would lose their senses.

53   *rage* : madness.

56   *spit*: pierce.
57   *Stay*: stop.

Seeking out Romeo, that did spit his body
Upon a rapier's point. Stay, Tybalt, stay!
Romeo, Romeo, Romeo!
Here's drink—I drink to thee!

[*She falls upon her bed within the curtains*

Act 4   Scene 4

The Capulet household is excited as
they prepare for the wedding. The
Nurse is sent to wake Juliet.

2   *pastry*: the room where pastry
(the 'bak'd meats' referred to in line 5)
is made.

4   *curfew bell*: the bell rang at night
(when the watch was set–see *3, 3, 147*)
and again in the morning (when the
watch went off duty).
5   *Angelica*: perhaps a teasing name
for the Nurse.
6   *spare not for cost*: don't think
about the expense.
    cot-quean: man who interferes in
the woman's job (i.e. housework).
8   *watching*: keeping awake.
9   *whit*: bit.
11   *mouse-hunt*: woman-chaser.
12   *watch*: prevent

13   *hood*: woman.

13s.d.   *spits*: iron bars for roasting meat
over fire.

Scene 4 *Verona: Capulet's house*

Enter Lady Capulet *and* Nurse

Lady Capulet
Hold, take these keys, and fetch more spices,
Nurse.
    Nurse
They call for dates and quinces in the pastry.

Enter Capulet

    Capulet
Come, stir, stir, stir! The second cock hath crow'd,
The curfew bell hath rung, 'tis three o'clock.
5 Look to the bak'd meats, good Angelica:
Spare not for cost.
    Nurse   Go, go, you cot-quean, go;
Get you to bed! Faith, you'll be sick tomorrow
For this night's watching.
    Capulet
No, not a whit. What, I have watch'd ere now
10 All night for lesser cause, and ne'er been sick.
    Lady Capulet
Ay, you have been a mouse-hunt in your time;
But I will watch you from such watching now.

[*Exeunt* Lady Capulet *and* Nurse

    Capulet
A jealous hood, a jealous hood!

Enter three or four Servants, *with spits,
logs, and baskets*

             Now, fellow, what is there?
    1 Servant
Things for the cook, sir, but I know not what.
    Capulet
15 Make haste, make haste. [*Exit* 1 Servant] Sirrah,
fetch drier logs:

Call Peter, he will show thee where they are.

2 Servant

I have a head, sir, that will find out logs,
And never trouble Peter for the matter.

Capulet

Mass, and well said; a merry whoreson, ha!
20 Thou shalt be loggerhead. [*Exit 2 Servant*] Good
    faith, 'tis day:
The County will be here with music straight,
For so he said he would.[*Music within*] I hear him
    near.
Nurse! Wife! What, ho! What, Nurse, I say!

Enter Nurse

Go waken Juliet, go and trim her up;
25 I'll go and chat with Paris. Hie, make haste,
Make haste! The bridegroom he is come already.
Make haste, I say.   [*Exeunt*

Scene 5 *Verona: Juliet's bedroom*

Enter Nurse

Nurse

Mistress! What, mistress! Juliet! Fast, I warrant
    her, she:
Why, lamb! why, lady! fie, you slug-a-bed!
Why, love, I say! Madam! sweet-heart! Why,
    bride!
What, not a word? You take your pennyworths
    now:
5 Sleep for a week; for the next night, I warrant,
The County Paris hath set up his rest
That you shall rest but little. God forgive me,
Marry, and amen, how sound is she asleep!
I needs must wake her. Madam, madam, madam!
10 Ay, let the County take you in your bed;
He'll fright you up, i' faith. Will it not be?
What, dress'd! And in your clothes, and down
    again!
I must needs wake you. Lady! lady! lady!
Alas! Alas! Help! help! my lady's dead!

---

17   I know how to find logs.

19   *Mass :* by the mass.
        whoreson : bastard.
20   *loggerhead :* blockhead.
21   *straight :* immediately.

24   *trim :* dress.

Act 4   Scene 5

The Nurse comes to wake Juliet and finds her apparently dead. The whole household (including the County Paris) join in lamentation.

1   *Fast :* i.e. fast asleep.
2   *slug-a-bed :* lazy person.
4   *You . . . now :* make sure that you get as much sleep now as you can.
5   *I warrant :* I'm sure.
6   *set up his rest :* made up his mind.
10   *take :* find.
11   *fright you up :* frighten you into getting up.
12   *down again :* lying down again (i.e. having got dressed).

15 O! well-a-day, that ever I was born.
     Some *aqua vitae*, ho! My lord! my lady!

    Enter Lady Capulet

  Lady Capulet
What noise is here?
  Nurse   O lamentable day!
  Lady Capulet
What is the matter?
  Nurse   Look, look! O heavy day!
  Lady Capulet
O me, O me! My child, my only life,
20 Revive, look up, or I will die with thee!
     Help, help! Call help.

    Enter Capulet

  Capulet
For shame, bring Juliet forth. Her lord is come.
  Nurse
She's dead, deceas'd, she's dead. Alack the day!
  Lady Capulet
Alack the day! She's dead, she's dead! She's dead!
  Capulet
25 Ha! Let me see her. Out, alas! She's cold;
     Her blood is settled, and her joints are stiff;
     Life and these lips have long been separated:
     Death lies on her like an untimely frost
     Upon the sweetest flower of all the field.
  Nurse
30 O lamentable day!
  Lady Capulet   O woeful time!
  Capulet
Death, that hath ta'en her hence to make me wail,
Ties up my tongue, and will not let me speak.

    Enter Friar Laurence *and* Paris, *with*
    Musicians
  Friar Laurence
Come, is the bride ready to go to church?
  Capulet
Ready to go, but never to return.
35 O son, the night before thy wedding-day

26 *is settled :* has ceased to flow.

28 *untimely :* early.

Hath Death lain with thy wife. There she lies,
Flower as she was, deflower'd by him.
Death is my son-in-law, Death is my heir;
My daughter he hath wedded. I will die,
40 And leave him all. Life, living, all is Death's!
  Paris
Have I thought long to see this morning's face,
And doth it give me such a sight as this?
  Lady Capulet
Accurs'd, unhappy, wretched, hateful day!
Most miserable hour, that e'er time saw
45 In lasting labour of his pilgrimage!
But one, poor one, one poor and loving child,
But one thing to rejoice and solace in,
And cruel death hath catch'd it from my sight!
  Nurse
O woe! O woeful, woeful, woeful day!
50 Most lamentable day, most woeful day,
That ever, ever, I did yet behold!
O day! O day! O day! O hateful day!
Never was seen so black a day as this:
O woeful day! O woeful day!
  Paris
55 Beguil'd, divorced, wronged, spited, slain!
Most detestable Death, by thee beguil'd,
By cruel cruel thee quite overthrown!
O love! O life! Not life, but love in death!
  Capulet
Despis'd, distressed, hated, martyr'd, kill'd!
60 Uncomfortable time, why cam'st thou now
To murder, murder our solemnity?
O child! O child! My soul, and not my child!
Dead art thou! Alack, my child is dead,
And with my child my joys are buried!
  Friar Laurence
65 Peace, ho! For shame! Confusion's cure lives not
In these confusions. Heaven and yourself
Had part in this fair maid; now heaven hath all,
And all the better is it for the maid.
Your part in her you could not keep from death,
70 But heaven keeps his part in eternal life.
The most you sought was her promotion,
For 'twas your heaven she should be advanc'd;

40   *living* : property.

41   *thought long* : waited for a long
time.
        this morning's face : the dawn of
this day.

45   *lasting* : everlasting.
        pilgrimage : progress (from year
to year).
47   *solace* : find solace.

58   *not . . . death* : Juliet is no longer
the County's 'life', but she is still his
love, even though she is dead.

60   *Uncomfortable* : grievous.
61   *solemnity* : ceremony.

65–6   *confusion . . . confusions* : the
remedy ('cure') for disaster
('Confusion') is not to be found in
these noisy outcries ('confusions').
67   *Had part* : shared.

71   *promotion* : i.e. to a higher social
status.

And weep ye now, seeing she is advanc'd
Above the clouds, as high as heaven itself?
75 O, in this love, you love your child so ill,
That you run mad, seeing that she is well.
She's not well married that lives married long;
But she's best married that dies married young.
Dry up your tears, and stick your rosemary
80 On this fair corse; and, as the custom is,
In all her best array bear her to church.
For though fond nature bids us all lament,
Yet nature's tears are reason's merriment.

Capulet

All things that we ordained festival,
85 Turn from their office to black funeral;
Our instruments to melancholy bells,
Our wedding cheer to a sad burial feast,
Our solemn hymns to sullen dirges change,
Our bridal flowers serve for a buried corse,
90 And all things change them to the contrary.

Friar Laurence

Sir, go you in; and, madam, go with him;
And go, Sir Paris. Every one prepare
To follow this fair corse unto her grave.
The heavens do lour upon you for some ill;
95 Move them no more by crossing their high will.
[*Exeunt* Capulet, Lady Capulet, Paris, *and* Friar

1 Musician

Faith, we may put up our pipes, and be gone.

Nurse

Honest good fellows, ah, put up, put up,
For, well you know, this is a pitiful case.   [*Exit*

1 Musician

Ay, by my troth, the case may be amended.

Enter Peter

Peter

100 Musicians, O, musicians, 'Heart's ease', 'Heart's
ease'! O, and ye will have me live, play 'Heart's ease'.

1 Musician

Why 'Heart's ease'?

Peter

O, musicians, because my heart itself plays 'My

79   *rosemary :* the herb of
remembrance, worn at weddings and
funerals.
80   *corse :* corpse.
82   *fond :* foolish.
83   Reason laughs at grief, although
grief is natural.

87   *cheer :* banquet.

90   *contrary :* opposite.

94   *lour :* frown.
95   *Move :* anger.
       crossing : frustrating.

96   *put up :* put away (in their cases).

98   *pitiful case :* sorrowful state of
affairs.

99   *case :* the Musician speaks as
though the Nurse refers to his
instrument-case.

100   *'Heart's ease' :* a popular tune of
the time.

104   *'My heart is full'* : the first line of
another popular song.
    dump : sad tune (a 'merry dump'
would be impossible).

111   *gleek* : gesture of scorn.
111–2 . *give you* : call you.
112   *minstrel* : a term of contempt (see
    3, 1, 44).
113   *serving-creature* : slave.
115   *pate* : head.
    crotchets : (a) musical notes; (b)
strange ideas.
115–6 *re . . . fa* : notes on the musical
    scale.
116   *note* : take notice of.
117   *And* : if.
118   Put your dagger away and use
some sense.

heart is full'; O, play me some merry dump to
105 comfort me.
    2 Musician
Not a dump we; 'tis no time to play now.
    Peter
You will not then?
    1 Musician
No.
    Peter
I will then give it you soundly.
    1 Musician
110 What will you give us?
    Peter
No money, on my faith, but the gleek; I will give
you the minstrel.
    1 Musician
Then will I give you the serving-creature.
    Peter
Then will I lay the serving-creature's dagger on
115 your pate. I will carry no crotchets: I'll *re* you, I'll
fa you. Do you note me?
    1 Musician
And you *re* us, and *fa* us, you note us.
    2 Musician
Pray you, put up your dagger, and put out your wit.

119   *have at you :* I attack you.
       dry-beat : beat without drawing
blood.
122ff '*When griping . . . :* the opening
of a lyric by Richard Edwardes
(1523–66).

126   *Catling :* the string of a small
lute.

128   *Prates :* nonsense (literally, 'he
chatters').
       Rebeck : a kind of fiddle.
129   *sound for :* play for.

131   *Soundpost :* wooden peg fixed
below the bridge of a violin.

133   *cry you mercy :* sorry.
       say : speak.

137   *redress :* comfort.

139   *jack :* scoundrel.
       tarry : wait for.
140   *stay dinner :* stay to dinner.

Peter
Then have at you with my wit! I will dry-beat you
120 with an iron wit, and put up my iron dagger.
Answer me like men:

    When griping griefs the heart doth wound,
      And doleful dumps the mind oppress,
    Then music with her silver sound—

125 Why 'silver sound'? why 'music with her silver
sound'? What say you, Simon Catling?
        1 Musician
Marry, sir, because silver hath a sweet sound.
        Peter
Prates. What say you, Hugh Rebeck?
        2 Musician
I say 'silver sound' because musicians sound for
130 silver.
        Peter
Prates too! What say you, James Soundpost?
        3 Musician
Faith, I know not what to say.
        Peter
O, I cry you mercy! You are the singer; I will say
for you. It is, 'music with her silver sound', because
135 musicians have no gold for sounding:
      Then music with her silver sound
        With speedy help doth lend redress.   [*Exit*
        1 Musician
What a pestilent knave is this same!
        2 Musician
Hang him, jack! Come, we'll in here; tarry for the
140 mourners, and stay dinner.   [*Exeunt*

Act 5

Act 5 Scene 1

In Mantua, Romeo hears news of
Juliet's death. His mind is made up.

1 Sleep flatters by making us
believe (in dreams) that what we long
for is real.

2 *presage :* foretell.
at hand : close by.

3 *My bosom's lord :* i.e. love.
throne : Romeo's heart.

4 *spirit :* cheerfulness.

11 *but love's shadows :* the mere
shadows (dreams) of love.

11s.d. *booted :* i.e. to show that he has
just been travelling.

18 *Capel's :* Capulet's
21 *presently :* immediately.
took post : travelled with post-
horses (these were changed at inns
along the route, and so were always
fresh and could travel faster.)

23 *office :* duty.

Scene 1 *Mantua*

Enter Romeo

Romeo
If I may trust the flattering truth of sleep,
My dreams presage some joyful news at hand.
My bosom's lord sits lightly in his throne,
And all this day an unaccustom'd spirit
5 Lifts me above the ground with cheerful thoughts.
I dreamt my lady came and found me dead—
Strange dream, that gives a dead man leave to
think—
And breath'd such life with kisses in my lips,
That I reviv'd and was an emperor.
10 Ah me! How sweet is love itself possess'd,
When but love's shadows are so rich in joy!

Enter Balthasar, *booted*
News from Verona! How now, Balthasar?
Dost thou not bring me letters from the friar?
How doth my lady? Is my father well?
15 How doth my lady Juliet? That I ask again,
For nothing can be ill if she be well.

Balthasar
Then she is well, and nothing can be ill;
Her body sleeps in Capel's monument,
And her immortal part with angels lives.
20 I saw her laid low in her kindred's vault,
And presently took post to tell it you.
O pardon me for bringing these ill news,
Since you did leave it for my office, sir.

24   *e'en :* even, indeed.
      I defy you, stars : Romeo will not wait for the stars (fate or fortune) to dictate what he should do now. He will act in defiance.

28   *import :* threaten.

35   *Let's see for means :* let me think what I can use.

38   *late :* recently.
      noted : noticed.
39   *weeds :* clothes.
      overwhelming : overhanging.
40   *Culling of simples :* gathering herbs.

45   *account :* number.
46   *earthen :* earthenware.
      bladders : used for storing liquids.
47   *packthread :* strong string.
      cakes of roses : rose-petals compressed into cakes and used as perfumes.
51   *present death :* punishable by instant death.
52   *caitiff :* miserable.
53   *forerun :* anticipate.

Romeo
Is it e'en so? Then I defy you, stars!
25 Thou know'st my lodging: get me ink and paper,
And hire post-horses. I will hence to-night.
    Balthasar
I do beseech you, sir, have patience:
Your looks are pale and wild, and do import
Some misadventure.
    Romeo   Tush, thou art deceiv'd;
30 Leave me, and do the thing I bid thee do.
Hast thou no letters to me from the friar?
    Balthasar
No, my good lord.
    Romeo   No matter; get thee gone,
And hire those horses: I'll be with thee straight.
                      [*Exit* Balthasar
Well, Juliet, I will lie with thee tonight.
35 Let's see for means. O mischief, thou art swift
To enter in the thoughts of desperate men.
I do remember an apothecary,
And hereabouts he dwells, which late I noted,
In tatter'd weeds, with overwhelming brows,
40 Culling of simples. Meagre were his looks,
Sharp misery had worn him to the bones;
And in his needy shop a tortoise hung,
An alligator stuff'd, and other skins
Of ill-shap'd fishes; and about his shelves
45 A beggarly account of empty boxes,
Green earthen pots, bladders, and musty seeds,
Remnants of packthread, and old cakes of roses,
Were thinly scatter'd, to make up a show.
Noting this penury, to myself I said
50 'And if a man did need a poison now,
(Whose sale is present death in Mantua)
Here lives a caitiff wretch would sell it him.'
O this same thought did but forerun my need,
And this same needy man must sell it me.
55 As I remember, this should be the house:
Being holiday, the beggar's shop is shut.
What ho! Apothecary!

Enter Apothecary

Apothecary   Who calls so loud?

Romeo

Come hither, man. I see that thou art poor.
Hold, there is forty ducats; let me have
60 A dram of poison, such soon-speeding gear
As will disperse itself through all the veins
That the life-weary taker may fall dead,
And that the trunk may be discharg'd of breath
As violently as hasty powder fir'd
65 Doth hurry from the fatal cannon's womb.

Apothecary

Such mortal drugs I have; but Mantua's law
Is death to any he that utters them.

Romeo

Art thou so bare, and full of wretchedness,
And fear'st to die? Famine is in thy cheeks,
70 Need and oppression starveth in thine eyes,
Contempt and beggary hangs upon thy back;
The world is not thy friend nor the world's law:
The world affords no law to make thee rich;
Then be not poor, but break it, and take this.

Apothecary

75 My poverty, but not my will, consents.

Romeo

I pay thy poverty, and not thy will.

59   *forty ducats :* a substantial sum—
the ducat was a small gold coin.
60   *soon-speeding :* quick-acting.
gear : stuff.

63   *trunk :* body.
64   *fir'd :* when it is set on fire.

66   *mortal :* lethal.
67   *utters :* dispenses, offers for sale.

70   *oppression :* distress.
starveth in thine eyes : show in the
hungry look in your eyes.
71   *Contempt and beggary :* despised
poverty.
hangs upon thy back : i.e. with his
clothes.

Apothecary
Put this in any liquid thing you will,
And drink it off; and, if you had the strength
Of twenty men, it would dispatch you straight.
Romeo
80 There is thy gold—worse poison to men's souls,
Doing more murder in this loathsome world
Than these poor compounds that thou mayst not
   sell.
I sell thee poison, thou hast sold me none.
Farewell; buy food, and get thyself in flesh.
85 Come, cordial and not poison, go with me
To Juliet's grave, for there I must use thee.

[*Exeunt*

79   *dispatch* : kill.

84   *get thyself in flesh* : grow fat.
85   *cordial* : a restorative medicine
for the heart.

Scene 2   *Verona : Friar Laurence's cell*

Enter Friar John

Friar John
Holy Franciscan friar! Brother, ho!

Enter Friar Laurence

Friar Laurence
This same should be the voice of Friar John.
Welcome from Mantua: what says Romeo?
Or, if his mind be writ, give me his letter.
Friar John
5 Going to find a bare-foot brother out,
One of our order, to associate me,
Here in this city visiting the sick,
And finding him, the searchers of the town,
Suspecting that we both were in a house
10 Where the infectious pestilence did reign,
Seal'd up the doors, and would not let us forth;
So that my speed to Mantua there was stay'd.
Friar Laurence
Who bore my letter, then, to Romeo?
Friar John
I could not send it—here it is again—
15 Nor get a messenger to bring it thee,
So fearful were they of infection.

Act 5   Scene 2
Friar Laurence learns of the
misfortune that has delayed his letter to
Romeo. He and Friar John hurry to the
vault of the Capulets.

4   *his mind be writ* : he has written
down his thoughts.
5   *bare-foot brother* : i.e. another
Franciscan friar; members of the Order
always travelled bare-foot, and in pairs.
6   *associate* : accompany.
8   *searchers of the town* : the town's
health officials, whose job was to view
all dead bodies and cases of infectious
illness. If the plague ('infectious
pestilence') was suspected, any contacts
were put under house-arrest until the
period of infection was over.

Friar Laurence
Unhappy fortune! By my brotherhood,
The letter was not nice, but full of charge,
Of dear import; and the neglecting it
20 May do much danger. Friar John, go hence;
Get me an iron crow, and bring it straight
Unto my cell.
  Friar John
Brother, I'll go and bring it thee.   [*Exit*
  Friar Laurence
Now must I to the monument alone;
Within this three hours will fair Juliet wake.
25 She will beshrew me much that Romeo
Hath had no notice of these accidents;
But I will write again to Mantua,
And keep her at my cell till Romeo come.
Poor living corse, clos'd in a dead man's tomb!
                                          [*Exit*

18 *nice :* formal.
    charge : instructions.
19 *import :* importance.

21 *crow :* crowbar.
    straight : immediately.

23 *must I :* I must go.

25 *beshrew :* curse.
26 *accidents :* happenings.

Act 5   Scene 3

Paris has come to say prayers at Juliet's tomb. He hides when he hears footsteps, but comes out of hiding when Romeo starts to force open the vault. Romeo and Paris fight; Paris is killed. When Romeo finds Juliet's body he laments for a time before drinking the drug which he brought from the apothecary in Mantua. Friar Laurence is too late to save him and Juliet, when she wakes, sees the dead body of her husband. She too kills herself. Paris's Page has called the Watch, and the families of the two lovers have been sent for. Friar Laurence explains all.

1   *aloof :* at a distance.
2   *would not :* do not want to.
3   *all along :* on the ground.
4   *hollow :* because of the graves.
10 *stand :* remain.
13 *canopy :* the covering of the four-poster bed (see illustration, p. 8).
14 *sweet :* scented.
    dew : sprinkle.
15 *wanting that :* if I don't have the 'sweet water'.

Scene 3 *Verona : the churchyard*

Enter Paris, *and his* Page, *bearing flowers, scented water, and a torch*

  Paris
Give me thy torch, boy. Hence, and stand aloof;
Yet put it out, for I would not be seen.
Under yon yew trees lay thee all along,
Holding thy ear close to the hollow ground:
5 So shall no foot upon the churchyard tread,
Being loose, unfirm with digging up of graves,
But thou shalt hear it: whistle then to me,
As signal that thou hear'st something approach.
Give me those flowers. Do as I bid thee; go.
  Page
10 [*Aside*] I am almost afraid to stand alone
Here in the churchyard; yet I will adventure.
                                       [*Retires*
  Paris
Sweet flower, with flowers thy bridal bed I strew.
O woe, thy canopy is dust and stones;
Which with sweet water nightly I will dew,
15 Or, wanting that, with tears distill'd by moans;

16   *obsequies :* funeral observances.

The obsequies that I for thee will keep
Nightly shall be to strew thy grave and weep.
                              [*The* Page *whistles*
The boy gives warning something doth approach.
What cursed foot wanders this way tonight,
20 To cross my obsequies and true love's rite?
What, with a torch? Muffle me, night, awhile.
                                        [*Retires*

Enter Romeo *and* Balthasar, *with a torch,*
mattock, &c.

          Romeo
Give me that mattock and the wrenching iron.
Hold, take this letter. Early in the morning
See thou deliver it to my lord and father.

26   *all aloof :* well away.

25 Give me the light. Upon thy life I charge thee,
Whate'er thou hear'st or seest, stand all aloof,
And do not interrupt me in my course.
Why I descend into this bed of death
Is partly to behold my lady's face,
30 But chiefly to take thence from her dead finger
A precious ring, a ring that I must use
In dear employment. Therefore hence, be gone:

33   *jealous :* suspicious.

But if thou, jealous, dost return to pry
In what I farther shall intend to do,
35 By heaven, I will tear thee joint by joint,

36   *hungry :* i.e. wanting more
bodies.

And strew this hungry churchyard with thy limbs.
The time and my intents are savage-wild,
More fierce and more inexorable far

39   *empty : hungry.*

Than empty tigers or the roaring sea.
          Balthasar
40 I will be gone, sir, and not trouble you.
          Romeo

41   *So :* in this way.

So shalt thou show me friendship. Take thou that:
Live, and be prosperous; and farewell, good fellow.
          Balthasar

43   *For all this same :* despite what he
says.

[*Aside*] For all this same, I'll hide me here about:
His looks I fear, and his intents I doubt.   [*Retires*
          Romeo

45   *maw :* stomach (i.e. the vault).

45 Thou detestable maw, thou womb of death,
Gorg'd with the dearest morsel of the earth,
Thus I enforce thy rotten jaws to open,
                    [*He starts to open the tomb*

And, in despite, I'll cram thee with more food!

Paris

This is that banish'd haughty Montague,
50 That murder'd my love's cousin, with which grief
It is supposed the fair creature died;
And here is come to do some villainous shame
To the dead bodies. I will apprehend him.

[*Comes forward*

Stop thy unhallow'd toil, vile Montague,
55 Can vengeance be pursu'd further than death?
Condemned villain, I do apprehend thee.
Obey, and go with me; for thou must die.

Romeo

I must, indeed; and therefore came I hither.
Good gentle youth, tempt not a desperate man;
60 Fly hence and leave me. Think upon these gone;
Let them affright thee. I beseech thee, youth,
Put not another sin upon my head
By urging me to fury. O, be gone:
By heaven, I love thee better than myself.
65 For I come hither arm'd against myself:
Stay not, be gone: live, and hereafter say
A madman's mercy bade thee run away.

Paris

I do defy thy conjuration,
And apprehend thee for a felon here.

Romeo

70 Wilt thou provoke me? Then have at thee, boy!

[*They fight*

Page

O Lord, they fight! I will go call the watch. [*Exit*

Paris

[*Falls*] O, I am slain!—If thou be merciful,
Open the tomb, lay me with Juliet.   [*Dies*

Romeo

In faith, I will. Let me peruse this face.
75 Mercutio's kinsman, noble County Paris!
What said my man when my betossed soul
Did not attend him as we rode? I think
He told me Paris should have married Juliet:
Said he not so? Or did I dream it so?
80 Or am I mad, hearing him talk of Juliet,
To think it was so? O give me thy hand,

---

48   *in despite :* in defiance.
     more food : i.e. his own body.

56   *apprehend :* arrest.

60   *these gone :* the dead bodies in the
churchyard.
61   *affright :* frighten.

68   *defy thy conjuration :* reject your
appeal.
69   *for a felon :* as a criminal.

76   *betossed :* disturbed.
77   *attend :* listen to.

82   *One writ with me* : one whose
name has been written with mine.

84   *lantern* : the architectural name
for a room filled with light.

86   *feasting presence* : banqueting
chamber.

87   *Death* : Romeo addresses the
body of Paris. He refers to himself
when he speaks of the 'dead man'.

89   *keepers* : prison warders, sick-bed
attendants.

90   *lightning* : i.e. of the spirits.

94   *ensign* : flag; as long as beauty's
red flag is seen in Juliet's cheeks and
lips, the white flag of death cannot be
raised ('advanc'd').

103   *unsubstantial* : bodiless.

110   *set . . . rest* : remain here for ever.
111   *Shake the yoke* : resist the
domination.
       inauspicious stars : unfavourable
Fortune.

115   An everlasting bargain with
Death, who finally takes possession of
(engrosses) everything.
116   *conduct* : guide.
118   *bark* : boat.

One writ with me in sour misfortune's book.
I'll bury thee in a triumphant grave—
                              [*He opens the tomb*
      A grave? O no, a lantern, slaughter'd youth,
85 For here lies Juliet, and her beauty makes
      This vault a feasting presence full of light.
      Death, lie thou there, by a dead man interr'd,
                              [*Laying* Paris *in the tomb*
      How oft when men are at the point of death
      Have they been merry! which their keepers call
90 A lightning before death. O how may I
      Call this a lightning? O my love, my wife!
      Death, that hath suck'd the honey of thy breath,
      Hath had no power yet upon thy beauty.
      Thou art not conquer'd; beauty's ensign yet
95 Is crimson in thy lips and in thy cheeks,
      And death's pale flag is not advanced there.
      Tybalt, liest thou there in thy bloody sheet?
      O what more favour can I do to thee,
      Than with that hand that cut thy youth in twain
100 To sunder his that was thine enemy?
      Forgive me, cousin! Ah, dear Juliet,
      Why art thou yet so fair? Shall I believe
      That unsubstantial death is amorous,
      And that the lean abhorred monster keeps
105 Thee here in dark to be his paramour?
      For fear of that I still will stay with thee,
      And never from this palace of dim night
      Depart again. Here, here will I remain
      With worms that are thy chambermaids; O here
110 Will I set up my everlasting rest,
      And shake the yoke of inauspicious stars
      From this world-wearied flesh. Eyes, look your
           last!
      Arms, take your last embrace! And lips, O you
      The doors of breath, seal with a righteous kiss
115 A dateless bargain to engrossing death!
      Come, bitter conduct, come, unsavoury guide!
      Thou desperate pilot, now at once run on
      The dashing rocks thy sea-sick weary bark!
      Here's to my love![*Drinks*] O true apothecary,
120 Thy drugs are quick. Thus with a kiss I die.
                              [*Dies*

Enter Friar Laurence *with a lantern, crowbar, and spade*

Friar Laurence

Saint Francis be my speed! How oft tonight
Have my old feet stumbled at graves! Who's there?

Balthasar

Here's one, a friend, and one that knows you well.

Friar Laurence

Bliss be upon you! Tell me, good my friend,
125 What torch is yon, that vainly lends his light
To grubs and eyeless skulls? As I discern,
It burneth in the Capels' monument.

Balthasar

It doth so, holy sir; and there's my master,
One that you love   Who is it?

Friar Laurence   **Balthasar**   Romeo.

Friar Laurence

130 How long hath he been there?

Balthasar   Full half an hour.

Friar Laurence

Go with me to the vault.

Balthasar   I dare not, sir.

My master knows not but I am gone hence;
And fearfully did menace me with death
If I did stay to look on his intents.

Friar Laurence

135 Stay then, I'll go alone. Fear comes upon me;
O much I fear some ill unthrifty thing.

Balthasar

As I did sleep under this yew-tree here,
I dreamt my master and another fought,
And that my master slew him.

Friar Laurence   Romeo!

140 Alack, alack! What blood is this which stains
The stony entrance of this sepulchre?
What means these masterless and gory swords
To lie discolour'd by this place of peace?

                                   [*Enters the tomb*

Romeo! O, pale! Who else? What! Paris too?
145 And steep'd in blood? Ah, what an unkind hour
Is guilty of this lamentable chance.
The lady stirs.   [*Juliet wakes*

---

121   *speed* : haste.
122   *stumbled at* : stumbled over; this was regarded as a bad omen..

125   *vainly* : in vain.

127   *Capels'* : Capulets'.

132   *knows . . . hence* : thinks I have gone away.

136   *ill unthrifty* : evil and unfortunate.

142   *What means* : why do?
       masterless : without owners.

Juliet

148 *comfortable :* giving spiritual
comfort.

O, comfortable friar! Where is my lord?
I do remember well where I should be,
150 And there I am. Where is my Romeo?

[*Noise within*

Friar Laurence

I hear some noise. Lady, come from that nest
Of death, contagion, and unnatural sleep.
A greater power than we can contradict
Hath thwarted our intents: come, come away.
155 Thy husband in thy bosom there lies dead;
And Paris too. Come, I'll dispose of thee
Among a sisterhood of holy nuns.
Stay not to question, for the watch is coming;
Come, go, good Juliet.—[*Noise again*] I dare no
longer stay.

Juliet

160 Go, get thee hence, for I will not away.

[*Exit* Friar Laurence

What's here? A cup, clos'd in my true love's hand?

162 *timeless :* untimely.

Poison, I see, hath been his timeless end.
O churl! Drunk all, and left no friendly drop
To help me after! I will kiss thy lips;
165 Haply, some poison yet doth hang on them,
To make me die with a restorative.   [*Kisses him*
Thy lips are warm!

1 Watchman

[*Within*] Lead, boy: which way?

Juliet

Yea, noise? Then I'll be brief. O happy dagger!

[*Snatching* Romeo's *dagger*

This is thy sheath; [*Stabs herself*] there rust, and
let me die.   [*Falls on* Romeo's *body and dies.*

Enter Watchmen, *with the* Page *of* Paris

Page

170 This is the place—there where the torch doth burn.

1 Watchman

The ground is bloody. Search about the churchyard.

172 *attach :* arrest.

Go, some of you; whoe'er you find, attach.

[*Exeunt some of the* Watchmen

Pitiful sight! Here lies the County slain,
And Juliet bleeding, warm, and newly dead,
175 Who here hath lain these two days buried.
Go, tell the Prince, run to the Capulets,
Raise up the Montagues; some others search.

[*Exeunt other* Watchmen

We see the ground whereon these woes do lie;
But the true ground of all these piteous woes
180 We cannot without circumstance descry.

178   *the ground :* the earth.
179   *the true ground :* the real cause.
180   *circumstance :* detailed
        knowledge.
        descry : perceive.

Enter some of the Watchmen, *with* Balthasar

2 Watchman
Here's Romeo's man; we found him in the churchyard.
1 Watchman
Hold him in safety, till the Prince come hither.

Enter other Watchmen, *with* Friar Laurence

3 Watchman
Here is a friar, that trembles, sighs, and weeps.
We took this mattock and this spade from him,
185 As he was coming from this churchyard side.
1 Watchman
A great suspicion: stay the friar too.

Enter the Prince *and* Attendants

Prince
What misadventure is so early up,
That calls our person from our morning rest?

Enter Capulet, Lady Capulet, *and Others*

Capulet
What should it be, that they so shriek abroad?
Lady Capulet
190 The people in the street cry 'Romeo',
Some 'Juliet', and some 'Paris'; and all run
With open outcry toward our monument.
Prince
What fear is this which startles in our ears?
2 Watchman
Sovereign, here lies the County Paris slain;

195 And Romeo dead; and Juliet, dead before,
Warm and new kill'd.

Prince

Search, seek, and know how this foul murder
comes.

1 Watchman

Here is a friar, and slaughter'd Romeo's man,
With instruments upon them fit to open
200 These dead men's tombs.

Capulet

O heaven!—O wife, look how our daughter bleeds!
This dagger hath mista'en!—for, lo, his house
Is empty on the back of Montague,
And it mis-sheathed in my daughter's bosom.

Lady Capulet

205 O me! This sight of death is as a bell,
That warns my old age to a sepulchre.

Enter Montague *and Others*

Prince

Come, Montague: for thou art early up,
To see thy son and heir now early down.

Montague

Alas my liege, my wife is dead tonight!
210 Grief of my son's exile hath stopp'd her breath.
What further woe conspires against mine age?

Prince

Look, and thou shalt see.

Montague

O thou untaught! What manners is in this,
To press before thy father to a grave?

Prince

215 Seal up the mouth of outrage for a while,
Till we can clear these ambiguities,
And know their spring, their head, their true
descent.
And then will I be general of your woes,
And lead you, even to death. Meantime forbear,
220 And let mischance be slave to patience.
Bring forth the parties of suspicion.

Friar Laurence

I am the greatest, able to do least,
Yet most suspected, as the time and place

202   *house :* sheath.

206   *warns :* summons.

209   *is dead tonight :* died last night.

213   *untaught :* Montague's own death should have taught his son to die.
214   *press :* push.

215   *mouth of outrage :* your expressions of violent grief.

218   *general :* leader.

220   *let . . . patience :* let patience rule over misfortune.
221   *parties of suspicion :* suspects.
222   I am the biggest suspect, though the least powerful.

224   *make :* argue.
225   *impeach :* accuse.
    purge : clear from guilt.

228   *my short date of breath :* the short
time that I have left to live.

232   *stol'n :* secret.

237   *perforce :* by force.

242   *tutor'd :* taught.

244   *wrought on :* produced in.
245   *form :* appearance.
246   *as :* on.

254   *closely :* secretly.

Doth make against me, of this direful murder;
225 And here I stand, both to impeach and purge
Myself condemned and myself excus'd.

Prince

Then say at once what thou dost know in this.

Friar Laurence

I will be brief, for my short date of breath
Is not so long as is a tedious tale.
230 Romeo, there dead, was husband to that Juliet;
And she, there dead, that Romeo's faithful wife.
I married them, and their stol'n marriage-day
Was Tybalt's doomsday, whose untimely death
Banish'd the new-made bridegroom from this city;
235 For whom, and not for Tybalt, Juliet pin'd.
You, to remove that siege of grief from her,
Betroth'd, and would have married her perforce
To County Paris. Then comes she to me,
And with wild looks bid me devise some mean
240 To rid her from this second marriage,
Or in my cell there would she kill herself.
Then gave I her—so tutor'd by my art—
A sleeping potion; which so took effect
As I intended, for it wrought on her
245 The form of death. Meantime I writ to Romeo
That he should hither come as this dire night
To help to take her from her borrow'd grave,
Being the time the potion's force should cease.
But he which bore my letter, Friar John,
250 Was stay'd by accident, and yesternight
Return'd my letter back. Then all alone
At the prefixed hour of her waking,
Came I to take her from her kindred's vault,
Meaning to keep her closely at my cell,
255 Till I conveniently could send to Romeo.
But, when I came, some minute ere the time
Of her awakening, here untimely lay
The noble Paris and true Romeo dead.
She wakes; and I entreated her come forth,
260 And bear this work of heaven with patience.
But then a noise did scare me from the tomb,
And she, too desperate, would not go with me,
But, as it seems, did violence on herself.
All this I know; and to the marriage

265	*is privy* : shared the secret.
266	*Miscarried* : went wrong.

269	*still* : always.

272	*in post* : in haste.

275	*going* : as he was going.

279	*what made your master* : what was your master doing?

282	*Anon* : presently.

293	*winking at* : closing my eyes to.
294	*a brace of kinsmen* : i.e. Mercutio and Paris.

296	*jointure* : dowry; all that Capulet can offer now is to join hands with Old Montague.

300	*figure* : statue.
	rate : value.

265 Her Nurse is privy: and, if aught in this
Miscarried by my fault, let my old life
Be sacrific'd, some hour before his time,
Unto the rigour of severest law.
Prince
We still have known thee for a holy man.
270 Where's Romeo's man? What can he say to this?
Balthasar
I brought my master news of Juliet's death;
And then in post he came from Mantua
To this same place, to this same monument.
This letter he early bid me give his father,
275 And threaten'd me with death, going in the vault,
If I departed not and left him there.
Prince
Give me the letter; I will look on it.
Where is the County's page that rais'd the watch?
Sirrah, what made your master in this place?
Page
280 He came with flowers to strew his lady's grave,
And bid me stand aloof, and so I did.
Anon comes one with light to ope the tomb,
And by and by my master drew on him.
And then I ran away to call the watch.
Prince
285 This letter doth make good the friar's words—
Their course of love, the tidings of her death.
And here he writes that he did buy a poison
Of a poor 'pothecary, and therewithal
Came to this vault to die, and lie with Juliet.
290 Where be these enemies?—Capulet! Montague!
See what a scourge is laid upon your hate,
That heaven finds means to kill your joys with love;
And I, for winking at your discords too,
Have lost a brace of kinsmen. All are punished.
Capulet
295 O brother Montague, give me thy hand:
This is my daughter's jointure, for no more
Can I demand.
Montague   But I can give thee more.
For I will raise her statue in pure gold,
That whiles Verona by that name is known,
300 There shall no figure at such rate be set
As that of true and faithful Juliet.

Capulet

302   *Romeo's :* i.e. Romeo's statue.   As rich shall Romeo's by his lady's lie;
303   *sacrifices :* victims.   Poor sacrifices of our enmity!

Prince

304   *glooming :* gloomy.   A glooming peace this morning with it brings;
                                    305   The sun for sorrow will not show his head.
                                          Go hence, to have more talk of these sad things:
                                          Some shall be pardon'd, and some punished:
                                              For never was a story of more woe
                                              Than this of Juliet and her Romeo.

                                                                    [*Exeunt*

Appendix

Extracts from *Romeus and Juliet* by Arthur Brooke, 1562

Act 1, Scenes 2–5

    The weary winter nights restore the Christmas games,
And now the season doth invite to banquet townish dames.
And first in Capel's house, the chief of all the kin.
Spar'th for no cost, the wonted use of banquets to begin.
No lady fair or foul was in Verona town,
No knight or gentleman of high or low renown,
But Capulet himself hath bid unto his feast,
Or by his name in paper sent, appointed as a guest.
Young damsels thither flock, of bachelors a rout,
Not so much for the banquet's sake, as beauties to search out.
But not a Montague would enter at his gate—
For, as you heard, the Capulets and they were at debate—
Save Romeus, and he in mask with hidden face,
The supper done, with other five, did press into the place.
When they had masqu'd a while, with dames in courtly wise,
All did unmask, the rest did show them to their ladies' eyes.
But bashful Romeus with shamefast face forsook
The open press, and him withdrew into the chamber's nook.
But brighter than the sun, the waxen torches shone,
That maugre what he could, he was espied of everyone. . . .
The Capulets disdain the presence of their foe,
Yet they suppress their stirred ire, the cause I do not know.
Perhaps t'offend their guests the courteous knights are loth,
Perhaps they stay from sharp revenge, dreading the Prince's
        wrath;
Perhaps for that they sham'd to exercise their rage
Within their house, 'gainst one alone, and him of tender age.

                    (lines 155–172, 183–188)

Act 1,   Scene 5

As careful was the maid what way were best devise
To learn his name, that entertain'd her in so gentle wise,
Of whom her heart receiv'd so deep, so wide a wound.
An ancient dame she call'd to her, and in her ear gan round.
This old dame in her youth had nurs'd her with her milk,
With slender needle taught her sew, and how to spin with silk.
'What twain are those,' quoth she, 'which press unto the door,
Whose pages in their hand do bear two torches' light before?'
And then as each of them had of his household name,
So she him nam'd yet once again, the young and wily dame.
'And tell me who is he with visor in his hand,
That yonder doth in masquing weed beside the window stand?'
'His name is Romeus,' said she, 'a Montague,
Whose father's pride first stirr'd the strife which both your
          households rue.'
The word of 'Montague' her joys did overthrow,
And straight instead of happy hope, despair began to grow.
'What hap have I,' quoth she, 'to love my father's foe?
What, am I weary of my weal? What, do I wish my woe?'

                                        (lines 341–358)

Act 4,   Scene 3

'What do I know,' quoth she, 'if that this powder shall
Sooner or later than it should, or else not work at all?
And then my craft descried as open as the day,
The people's tale and laughing stock shall I remain for aye?'
'And what know I,' quoth she, 'if serpents odious,
And other beasts and worms that are of nature venomous,
That wonted are to lurk in dark cave underground,
And commonly (as I have heard) in dead men's tombs are found,
Shall harm me—yea or nay—where I shall lie as dead?
Or how shall I, that always have in so fresh air been bred,
Endure the loathsome stink of such an heaped store
Of carcasses not yet consum'd, and bones that long before
Entombed were, where I my sleeping-place shall have

Where all my ancestors do rest, my kindred's common grave?
Shall not the friar and my Romeus, when they come,
Find me (if I awake before) y-stifled in the tomb?
      And whilst she in these thoughts doth dwell somewhat too
         long,
The force of her imagining anon did wax so strong
That she surmis'd she saw out of the hollow vault
(A grisly thing to look upon) the carcass of Tybalt. . . .
Her dainty tender parts gan shiver all for dread,
Her golden hairs did stand upright upon her chillish head.
Then pressed with the fear that she there lived in,
A sweat as cold as mountain ice pierc'd through her tender skin,
That with the moisture hath wet every part of hers,
And more besides, she vainly thinks, whilst vainly thus she fears,
A thousand bodies dead have compass'd her about,
And lest they will dismember her, she greatly stands in doubt.
But when she felt her strength began to wear away,
By little and little, and in her heart her fear increased aye,
Dreading that weakness might, or foolish cowardice,
Hinder the execution of the purpos'd enterprise,
As she had frantic been, in haste the glass she caught.
And up she drank the mixture quite, without further thought.

(lines 2361–2380, 2387–2400)

Act 4,   Scene 1

      Now throughout Italy this common use they have,
That all the best of every stock are earthed in one grave,
For every household, if it be of any fame,
Doth build a tomb or dig a vault that bears the household's name;
Wherein (if any of that kindred hap to die)
They are bestow'd, else in the same no other corpse may lie.
The Capulets her corpse in such a one did lay,
Where Tybalt, slain of Romeus, was laid the other day.
An other use there is, that whosoever dies,
Borne to the church with open face, upon the bier he lies
In wonted weeds attir'd, not wrapp'd in winding-sheet.

(lines 2515–2525)

Act 5, Scene 3

     And lest that length of time might from our minds remove
The memory of so perfect, sound, and so approved love,
The bodies dead removed from the vault where they did die,
In stately tomb, on pillars great, of marble raise they high.
On every side above were set—and eke beneath—
Great store of cunning epitaphs, in honour of their death.
And even at this day the tomb is to be seen,
So that among the monuments that in Verona been,
There is no monument more worthy of the sight
Than is the tomb of Juliet, and Romeus her knight.

(lines 3011–3020)

Classwork and Examinations

The works of Shakespeare are studied all over the world, and this classroom edition is being used in many different countries. Teaching methods vary from school to school and there are many different ways of examining a student's work. Some teachers and examiners expect detailed knowledge of Shakespeare's text; others ask for imaginative involvement with his characters and their situations; and there are some teachers who want their students to share in the theatrical experience of directing and performing a play. Most people use a variety of methods. This section of the book offers a few suggestions for approaches to *Romeo and Juliet* which could be used in schools and colleges to help with students' understanding and *enjoyment* of the play.

> A Discussion
> B Character Study
> C Activities
> D Context Questions
> E Comprehension Questions
> F Essays
> G Projects

A Discussion

Talking about the play — about the issues it raises and the characters who are involved — is one of the most rewarding and pleasurable aspects of the study of Shakespeare. It makes sense to discuss each scene as it is read, sharing impressions — and perhaps correcting misapprehensions. It can be useful to compare aspects of this play with other fictions — plays, novels, films — or with modern life.

Suggestions

A1 What do you expect of *Romeo and Juliet* after reading the first Chorus ('Two households, both alike in dignity')? Is this Chorus really necessary?

A2   Romeo and Juliet are described as 'star-cross'd lovers'. Do you believe in 'the stars'? Do you read your horoscope?

A3   'A dog of the house of Montague stirs me' (*1*, 1, 7). Can you think of any other fictional — or real-life — situations of long-standing quarrels between families (or clans, or tribes)?

A4   Do you think parents should have any control over the marriages of their daughters or sons?

A5   Do you believe in love at first sight?

A6   Juliet asks 'What's in a name', and she observes 'That which we call a rose By any other name would smell as sweet' (*2*, 2, 43–4). Is there any 'magic' in a name?

A7   In most cultures, the proposal of marriage is made by the man. What is your opinion of this convention? (In the play, it is Juliet, not Romeo, who first speaks of 'marriage' — *2*, 2, 144).

A8   Romeo wants someone to advise him, and so he goes to Friar Laurence, the priest. Where could a modern young man (or woman) turn for advice?

A9   How would you, as director, handle the scene (*Act 4*, Scene 5) in which Juliet's Nurse and parents lament her death?

A10   What would be the advantages and disadvantages of a modern dress production of *Romeo and Juliet*?

B   Character Study

Shakespeare is famous for his creation of characters who seem like real people. We can judge their actions and we can try to understand their thoughts and feelings — just as we criticize and try to understand the people we know. As the play progresses, we learn to like or dislike, love or hate, them — just as though they lived in *our* world.

    Characters can be studied *from the outside*, by observing what they do, and listening sensitively to what they say. This is the scholar's method: the scholar — or any reader — has access to the whole play, and can see the function of every character within the whole scheme of that play.

    Another approach works *from the inside*, taking a single character and looking at the action and the other characters from his/her point of view. This is an actor's technique when creating a character — who can have only a partial view of what is going on — for performance; and it asks for a student's inventive imagination. The two methods — both useful in different ways — are really complementary to each other.

Suggestions

   a) from 'outside' the character

B1   Does Benvolio have a personality, or is the character merely functional?

B2   Compare and contrast
   a) Lady Capulet and Lady Montague.
   b) Romeo's father and Juliet's father.
   c) Mercutio and Benvolio.

B3   'We learn more about Tybalt from the remarks of other characters than from his own words and actions.' Is this true?

B4   Describe the character of Juliet's Nurse.

B5   Is Friar Laurence really a simple-minded busybody?

B6   'The character of Mercutio seems to be over-developed for his function in the play, whilst that of Paris is under-developed.' Do you agree with either part of this statement?

   b) from 'inside' a character

B7   Write a letter — or a poem — from Romeo to his first love, Rosaline.

B8   In the character of Juliet, write your personal diary at the end of *Act 1*, Scene 4, revealing your attitude to your mother and to your Nurse, and describing your feelings about the marriage that has been proposed for you.

B9   You are Lady Capulet. Tell us about your own early marriage ('I was your mother much upon these years That you are now a maid' — *1*, 3, 72–3), and your elderly husband (see *1*, 5, 21–40).

B10   In Juliet's diary, or in a letter to her girl-friend, describe
   a) the ball, and your first meeting with Romeo.
   b) your conversation with Romeo after the ball.
   c) the wedding in Friar Laurence's cell.

B11   In Romeo's personal diary
   a) compare Juliet with Rosaline.
   b) describe how you went as a 'gatecrasher' to the Capulet ball.
   c) record your conversation with Juliet after the ball.

B12 Write *Friar Laurence's Handbook of Herbal Remedies.*

B13 In the character of Tybalt, give a 'thumbnail sketch' of Romeo, Mercutio, and Benvolio.

B14 Write the 'letters' that Friar Laurence promises (*4, 2, 114*) to send to Romeo.

B15 As one of the musicians in *Act 4*, Scene 5, describe the scene that you have witnessed in the Capulet household.

C   Activities

These can involve two or more students, preferably working *away from* the desk or study-table and using gesture and position ('body-language') as well as speech. They can help students to develop a sense of drama and the dramatic aspects of Shakespeare's play — which was written to be *performed*, not studied in a classroom.

Suggestions

C1 Act the play — at least one or two scenes.

C2 The weather is very hot, and there is not much 'real' news for the media to report. Cover the 'Montague-Capulet Brawl' in *Act 1*, Scene 1 for the 'Verona News' — newspaper, radio, or television (with signing for deaf people, if possible). Interview as many as you can of the witnesses and those involved in the fighting, and get all the 'background' material that you can find.

C3 The County Paris has obviously been talking — and listening — to Juliet's father *before* the beginning of *Act 1*, Scene 2. Devise a new scene for them, so that Capulet can tell Paris — his would-be son-in-law — about the family feud and its latest outbreak.

C4 Using your own words, act out
   a) the flirtation in the ballroom (*1, 5, 93–109*).
   b) the 'balcony' scene after the ball (*Act 2*, Scene 2).
   c) the 'separation' (*3, 5, 1–59*).

C5 There is still not much 'real' news to report (the weather is even hotter), and interest in 'The Feuding Families' has spread outside Verona. Cover the fighting in *Act 3*, Scene 1 for the 'Northern Italy News'. Interview all spectators, and try to get comments from Benvolio and the relatives of the deceased. Get the 'sports editor' to explain the finer points of fencing, and ask the local priest for his views on duelling. Is there any official message from the Prince's palace?

C6 The night before she is to marry Paris, Juliet offers the Nurse's help to her mother:

> let the Nurse this night sit up with you;
> For, I am sure, you have your hands full all
> In this so sudden business.

4, 3, 10–12

Improvise the scene between Lady Capulet and the Nurse as they wait for the wedding-day to dawn.

C7 A Capulet wedding is obviously of great local interest in Verona. Send staff from all the media to cover it from the moment the bridegroom leaves his own house. Interview the musicians and cooks about their preparations. Try to get a word from the bride's mother, father, and Nurse. Has the bridegroom got anything to say? Is there a comment from the priest who will perform the ceremony? Can we expect a royal guest? Prepare headlines for the 'Verona News' so that you can publish/broadcast as soon as the event takes place.

C8 All the reporting staff are at hand [see above, C7] when Juliet's sudden death is discovered. React quickly to the changed circumstances — and get even better 'stories' for the local paper/programme! Expand the stories for readers/viewers of 'Northern Italy News'.

C9 Another news story has 'broken' in Verona: 'What should it be, that they so shriek abroad?' (5, 3, 189). Send the team of experienced reporters [from C7 and C8], or else send new reporters from the national papers and nation-wide programmes. Prepare translations and sub-titles for foreign publications/transmissions; and have the television coverage signed for the deaf.

C10 The Prince promises that 'Some shall be pardon'd, and some punished' (5, 3, 114). Hold a trial by jury.

D   Context Questions

In written examinations, these questions present you with short passages from the play, and ask you to explain them. They are intended to test your knowledge of the play and your understanding of its words. Usually you have to make a choice of passages: there may be five on the paper, and you are asked to choose three. Be very sure that you know exactly how many passages you must choose. Study the ones offered to you, and select those you feel most certain of. Make your answers accurate and concise — don't waste time writing more than the examiner is asking for.

D1   What, dares the slave
Come hither, cover'd with an antic face,
To fleer and scorn at our solemnity?
Now by the stock and honour of my kin,
To strike him dead I hold it not a sin.

   (i) Who is speaking, and who is the 'slave' that he speaks of?
  (ii) What is the 'solemnity' that he refers to?
 (iii) Who stops the speaker from fighting, and for what reasons?

D2 Now, afore God I am so vexed that every part about me quivers. Scurvy knave! Pray you, sir, a word — and as I told you, my young lady bid me inquire you out. What she bid me say I will keep to myself. But first let me tell ye, if ye should lead her in a fool's paradise, as they say, it were a very gross kind of behaviour, as they say; for the gentlewoman is young.

   (i) Who is speaking, and to whom?
  (ii) Who is the 'scurvy knave' that the speaker refers to, and who is the 'gentlewoman'?
 (iii) How old is she?
 (iv) What arrangements are made by the two characters involved here?

D3 It was the lark, the herald of the morn,
No nightingale. Look, love, what envious streaks
Do lace the severing clouds in yonder east.
Night's candles are burnt out, and jocund day
Stands tiptoe on the misty mountain tops.
I must be gone and live, or stay and die.

   (i) Who is speaking, and to whom?
  (ii) What are the two major events that happened on the previous day?
 (iii) Why will the speaker die if he remains where he is?

D4   she'll not be hit
With Cupid's arrow, she hath Dian's wit,
And in strong proof of chastity well arm'd
From love's weak childish bow she lives uncharm'd.

    (i) Who is speaking? What is the name of the lady he
       describes?
   (ii) Who is 'Cupid'?
  (iii) Is the lady hurt by Cupid's arrow?

D5 Art thou a man? Thy form cries out thou art.
Thy tears are womanish, thy wild acts denote
The unreasonable fury of a beast.
Unseemly woman in a seeming man,
And ill-beseeming beast in seeming both!

    (i) Who is the speaker? Whom does he address?
   (ii) What particular 'wild act' has been committed?
  (iii) What is the speaker's solution to the situation?

D6 Tut man, one fire burns out another's burning,
One pain is lessen'd by another's anguish;
Turn giddy, and be holp by backward turning.
One desperate grief cures with another's languish;
Take thou some new infection to thy eye
And the rank poison of the old will die.

    (i) Who is speaking and to whom does he speak?
   (ii) What is the 'infection' to which the speaker refers?
  (iii) How does the listener react to this advice?

E Comprehension Questions

These also present passages from the play and ask questions about
them, and again you often have a choice of passages. But the
extracts are much longer than those presented as context questions.
A detailed knowledge of the language of the play is asked for here,
and you must be able to express unusual or archaic phrases in your
own words; you may also be asked to comment critically on the
effectiveness of Shakespeare's language.

E1   *Capulet*

This night I hold an old accustom'd feast,
Whereto I have invited many a guest
Such as I love; and you among the store,
One more, most welcome, makes my number more.
At my poor house look to behold this night   5
Earth-treading stars that make dark heaven light.
Such comfort as do lusty young men feel
When well-apparell'd April on the heel
Of limping winter treads, even such delight
Among fresh female buds shall you this night   10
Inherit at my house. Hear all, all see,
And like her most whose merit most shall be:
Which, on more view of many, mine, being one,
May stand in number, though in reckoning none.

(i) Give the exact context of this passage.
(ii) Explain the meaning of 'old accustom'd' (line 1), and 'Earth-treading stars' (line 6).
(iii) In your own words express the idea contained in lines 13–14 ('Which . . . none').
(iv) Comment on the poetic qualities of the passage.

E2   *Romeo*

Arise, fair sun, and kill the envious moon,
Who is already sick and pale with grief,
That thou her maid art far more fair than she.
Be not her maid since she is envious;
Her vestal livery is but sick and green,   5
And none but fools do wear it; cast it off.
It is my lady. O, it is my love!
O that she knew she were!
She speaks, yet she says nothing: what of that?
Her eye discourses; I will answer it.   10
I am too bold; 'tis not to me she speaks:
Two of the fairest stars in all the heaven,
Having some business, do entreat her eyes
To twinkle in their spheres till they return.
What if her eyes were there, they in her head?   15
The brightness of her cheek would shame those stars
As daylight doth a lamp. Her eyes in heaven
Would through the airy region stream so bright
That birds would sing and think it were not night.

(i) Give the exact context of this speech.

(ii) What is meant by 'vestal livery' (line 5); 'Her eye discourses' (line 10); 'spheres' (line 14)?

(iii) Why is the moon called 'she' (line 1)?

(iv) Is this the language of real love?

Benvolio

E3 Madam, an hour before the worshipp'd sun
Peer'd forth the golden window of the east,
A troubled mind drove me to walk abroad
Where (underneath the grove of sycamore
That westward rooteth from this city side)   5
So early walking did I see your son.
Towards him I made, but he was ware of me,
And stole into the covert of the wood.
I, measuring his affections by my own,
Which then most sought where most might not be found,   10
Being one too many by my weary self,
Pursu'd my humour, not pursuing his,
And gladly shunn'd who gladly fled from me.

(i) Give the precise location of this speech.

(ii) What is meant by 'abroad' (line 3); 'westward rooteth' (line 5); and 'affections' (line 9)?

(iii) Put into your own words the idea expressed in line 10: 'Which then most sought where most might not be found'.

(iv) How would you describe Romeo's 'humour'?

F Essays

These will usually give you a specific topic to discuss, or perhaps a question that must be answered, in writing, *with a reasoned argument*. They *never* want you to tell the story of the play — so don't! Your examiner — or teacher — has read the play and does not need to be reminded of it. Relevant quotations will always help you to make your points more strongly.

F1 'All our sympathies are with Juliet because she receives very little help or guidance at home.' How true is this statement?

F2 Show how the feud between the Montagues and the Capulets includes the whole of the two households (not just the young men).

F3   How does Juliet's father change after the death of Tybalt?

F4   Compare and contrast Lady Capulet and Juliet's Nurse.

F5   Describe Romeo as a lover *before* and *after* he meets Juliet.

F6   Give an account of Friar Laurence and his function in the play.

F7   'It is too rash, too unadvis'd, too sudden'. Apply Juliet's words (2, 2, 118) to the action of the play.

F8   Who (in your opinion) is most to blame for this tragedy?

G   Projects

In some schools, students are asked to do more 'free-ranging' work, which takes them outside the text — but which should always be relevant to the play. Such Projects may demand skills other than reading and writing; design and artwork, for instance, may be involved. Sometimes a 'portfolio' of work is assembled over a considerable period of time; and this can be presented to the examiner as part of the student's work for assessment. The availability of resources will, obviously, do much to determine the nature of the Projects; but this is something that only the local teachers will understand. However, there is always help to be found in libraries, museums, and art galleries.

Suggested Topics

G1   Elizabethan Dancing.

G2   Elizabethan Weddings.

G3   Famous Actors and Actresses in *Romeo and Juliet*.

G4   *Romeo and Juliet* as Inspiration.

G5   The Art of Fencing.

Background

England c. 1595

When Shakespeare was writing *Romeo and Juliet,* most people believed that the sun went round the earth. They were taught that this was a divinely ordered scheme of things, and that — in England — God had instituted a Church and ordained a Monarchy for the right government of the land and the populace.

'The past is a foreign country; they do things differently there.'

L.P. Hartley

Government

For most of Shakespeare's life, the reigning monarch of England was Queen Elizabeth I. With her counsellors and ministers she governed the country (population about five million) from London, although fewer than half a million people inhabited the capital city. In the rest of the country, law and order were maintained by the land-owners and enforced by their deputies. The average man had no vote — and his wife had no rights at all.

Religion

At this time, England was a Christian country. All children were baptized, soon after they were born, into the Church of England; they were taught the essentials of the Christian faith, and instructed in their duty to God and to humankind. Marriages were performed, and funerals conducted, only by the licensed clergy and in accordance with the Church's rites and ceremonies. Attendance at divine service was compulsory; absences (without good — medical — reason) could be punished by fines. By such means, the authorities were able to keep some check on the populace — recording births, marriages, and deaths; being alert to any religious nonconformity, which could be politically dangerous; and ensuring a minimum of orthodox instruction through the official 'Homilies' which were regularly preached from the pulpits of all parish churches throughout the realm. Following Henry VIII's break away from the Church of Rome, all people in England were able to hear the church services *in their own language*. The Book of Common Prayer was used in every church, and an English translation of the Bible was read aloud in public. The Christian religion had never been so well taught before!

Education

School education reinforced the Church's teaching. From the age of four, boys might attend the 'petty school' (French *'petite école'*) to learn the rudiments of reading and writing along with a few prayers; some schools also included work with numbers. At the age of seven, the boy was ready for the grammar school (if his father was willing and able to pay the fees).

Here, a thorough grounding in Latin grammar was followed by translation work and the study of Roman authors, paying attention as much to style as to matter. The arts of fine writing were thus inculcated from early youth. A very few students proceeded to university; these were either clever scholarship boys, or else the sons of noblemen. Girls stayed at home, and acquired domestic and social skills — cooking, sewing, perhaps even music. The lucky ones might learn to read and write.

Language

At the start of the sixteenth century the English had a very poor opinion of their own language: there was little serious writing in English, and hardly any literature. Latin was the language of international scholarship, and Englishmen admired the eloquence of the Romans. They made many translations, and in this way they extended the resources of their own language, increasing its vocabulary and stretching its grammatical structures. French, Italian, and Spanish works were also translated, and — for the first time — there were English versions of the Bible. By the end of the century, English was a language to be proud of: it was rich in synonyms, capable of infinite variety and subtlety, and ready for all kinds of word-play — especially the *puns*, for which Elizabethan English is renowned.

Drama

The great art-form of the Elizabethan age was its drama. The Elizabethans inherited a tradition of play-acting from the Middle Ages, and they reinforced this by reading and translating the

Roman playwrights. At the beginning of the sixteenth century, plays were performed by groups of actors, all-male companies (boys acted the female roles) who travelled from town to town, setting up their stages in open places (such as inn-yards) or, with the permission of the owner, in the hall of some noble house. The touring companies continued, in the provinces, into the seventeenth century; but in London, in 1576, a new building was erected for the performance of plays. This was the Theatre, the first purpose-built playhouse in England. Other playhouses followed, (including Shakespeare's own theatre, the Globe) and the English drama reached new heights of eloquence.

There were those who disapproved, of course. The theatres, which brought large crowds together, could encourage the spread of disease — and dangerous ideas. During the summer, when the plague was at its worst, the playhouses were closed. A constant censorship was imposed, more or less severe at different times. The Puritan faction tried to close down the theatres, but — partly because there was royal favour for the drama, and partly because the buildings were outside the city limits — they did not succeed until 1642.

Theatre

From contemporary comments and sketches — most particularly a drawing by a Dutch visitor, Johannes de Witt — it is possible to form some idea of the typical Elizabethan playhouse for which most of Shakespeare's plays were written. Hexagonal in shape, it had three roofed galleries encircling an open courtyard. The plain, high stage projected into the yard, where it was surrounded by the audience of standing 'groundlings'. At the back were two doors for the actors' entrances and exits; and above these doors was a balcony — useful for a musicians' gallery or for the acting of scenes *above*. Over the stage was a thatched roof, supported on two pillars, forming a canopy — which seems to have been painted with the sun, moon, and stars for the 'heavens'. Underneath was space (concealed by curtaining) which could be used by characters ascending and descending through a trap-door in the stage. Costumes and properties were kept backstage, in the 'tiring house'. The actors dressed lavishly, often wearing the secondhand clothes bestowed by rich patrons. Stage properties were important for defining a location, but the dramatist's own words were needed to explain the time of day, since all performances took place in the early afternoon.

Selected Further Reading

Interesting work on *Romeo and Juliet* can be found in these books:

Bradley, A.C., *Shakespearian Tragedy*, (London, 1904).

Brooke, Nicholas, *Shakespeare's Early Tragedies*, (London, 1968).

Dusinberre, Juliet, *Shakespeare and the Nature of Women*, (London, 1975).

Edwards, Philip, *Shakespeare and the Confines of Art*, (London, 1968).

Everett, Barbara, '*Romeo and Juliet*: The Nurse's Story', *Critical Quarterly*, 14 (1972); reprinted in *Shakespeare's Wide and Universal Stage*, ed. C.B. Cox and D.J. Palmer, (Manchester, 1984).

Granville-Barker, Harley, *Prefaces to Shakespeare*, vol. 2, (London, 1930).

Kahn, Coppelia, 'Coming of age in Verona', *Modern Language Studies*, 8 (1977–8); reprinted in her book, *Man's Estate: Masculine Identity in Shakespeare*, (Berkeley and Los Angeles, Calif., 1981).

Mahood, Molly M., *Shakespeare's Wordplay*, (London, 1957).

Marsh, Derick R.C., *Passion Lends Them Power: A Study of Shakespeare's Love Tragedies*, (Sydney, 1976).

Muir, Kenneth, *The Sources of Shakespeare's Plays*, (London, 1977).

Further Background Reading

Blake, N.F., *Shakespeare's Language: an Introduction*, (Methuen, 1983).

Muir, K., and Schoenbaum, S., *A New Companion to Shakespeare Studies*, (Cambridge, 1971).

Schoenbaum, S., *William Shakespeare: A Documentary Life*, (Oxford, 1975).

Thomson, Peter, *Shakespeare's Theatre*, (Routledge and Kegan Paul, 1983).

William Shakespeare, 1564–1616

Elizabeth I was Queen of England when Shakespeare was born in 1564. He was the son of a tradesman who made and sold gloves in the small town of Stratford-upon-Avon, and he was educated at the grammar school in that town. Shakespeare did not go to university when he left school, but worked, perhaps, in his father's business. When he was eighteen he married Anne Hathaway, who became the mother of his daughter, Susanna, in 1583, and of twins in 1585.

There is nothing exciting, or even unusual, in this story; and from 1585 until 1592 there are no documents that can tell us anything at all about Shakespeare. But we have learned that in 1592 he was known in London, and that he had become both an actor and a playwright.

We do not know when Shakespeare wrote his first play, and indeed we are not sure of the order in which he wrote his works. If you look on page 134 at the list of his writings and their approximate dates, you will see how he started by writing plays on subjects taken from the history of England. No doubt this was partly because he was always an intensely patriotic man—but he was also a very shrewd business-man. He could see that the theatre audiences enjoyed being shown their own history, and it was certain that he would make a profit from this kind of drama.

The plays in the next group are mainly comedies, with romantic love stories of young people who fall in love with one another and, at the end of the play, marry and live happily ever after.

At the end of the sixteenth century the happiness disappears, and Shakespeare's plays become melancholy, bitter, and tragic. This change may have been caused by some sadness in the writer's life (one of his twins died in 1596). Shakespeare, however, was not the only writer whose works at this time were very serious. The whole of England was facing a crisis. Queen Elizabeth I was growing old. She was greatly loved, and the people were sad to think she must soon die; they were also afraid, for the Queen had never married, and so there was no child to succeed her.

When James I came to the throne in 1603, Shakespeare continued to write serious drama—the great tragedies and the plays based on Roman history (such as *Julius Caesar*) for which he is most famous. Finally, before he retired from the theatre, he wrote another set of comedies. These all have the same theme: they tell of happiness which is lost, and then found again.

Shakespeare returned from London to Stratford, his home town. He was rich and successful, and he owned one of the biggest houses in the town. He died in 1616.

Shakespeare also wrote two long poems, and a collection of sonnets. The sonnets describe two love-affairs, but we do not know who the lovers were. Although there are many public documents concerned with his career as a writer and a business-man, Shakespeare has hidden his personal life from us. A nineteenth-century poet, Matthew Arnold, addressed Shakespeare in a poem, and wrote 'We ask and ask—Thou smilest, and art still'.

There is not even a trustworthy portrait of the world's greatest dramatist.

Approximate order of composition of Shakespeare's works

Period	Comedies	History plays	Tragedies	Poems
I 1594	Comedy of Errors Taming of the Shrew Two Gentlemen of Verona Love's Labour's Lost	Henry VI, part 1 Henry VI, part 2 Henry VI, part 3 Richard III King John	Titus Andronicus	 Venus and Adonis Rape of Lucrece
II 1599	Midsummer Night's Dream Merchant of Venice Merry Wives of Windsor Much Ado About Nothing As You Like it	Richard II Henry IV, part 1 Henry IV, part 2 Henry V	Romeo and Juliet	Sonnets
III 1608	Twelfth Night Troilus and Cressida Measure for Measure All's Well That Ends Well		Julius Caesar Hamlet Othello Timon of Athens King Lear Macbeth Antony and Cleopatra Coriolanus	
IV 1613	Pericles Cymbeline The Winter's Tale The Tempest	Henry VIII		